THE
EVERYDAY
ENTREPRENEUR

HOW TO START AND GROW
YOUR ONLINE SIDE HUSTLE

B.M.HARGREAVES

First published in the UK in 2025

ISBN: 9798297486348

Disclaimers

The content within this publication is provided solely for general informational purposes and shall not be construed as constituting legal, financial, tax or other professional advice. The author expressly disclaims any and all liability for any direct, indirect, incidental, consequential or special damages, including but not limited to loss of profits, data or other intangible losses, arising out of or in connection with the use, reliance upon, or inability to use the information presented herein. Readers are strongly advised to seek independent counsel from duly qualified professionals to obtain advice tailored to their specific circumstances. By proceeding to read this guide, you acknowledge and agree that the author shall not be held responsible for any actions taken or decisions made based on the content herein.

References to third-party platforms and brands, are included herein solely for illustrative and informational purposes. The author is neither affiliated with, endorsed by, nor in any partnership with these entities, and the inclusion of such references does not imply any sponsorship, approval, or commercial relationship. The author makes no representations or warranties regarding the functionality, reliability, or suitability of these platforms for any purpose, and expressly disclaims liability for any adverse outcomes, financial losses, or other damages, whether direct or indirect, resulting from the use of or reliance upon these platforms. Readers engage with these third-party services at their own risk and are advised to review the terms of service, policies, and operational risks associated with each platform prior to use.

Financial outcomes and earnings derived from activities, as described within this publication, are subject to substantial variability due to factors

and educational purposes. Readers should note that individual outcomes may differ significantly, and circumstances at the time of writing may not reflect future conditions or their own personal situation. Economic factors, platform policies, tax laws and market dynamics are subject to change, and as such the relevance or accuracy of certain content may diminish over time. While every effort has been made to verify the information, the author does not accept responsibility for any errors, inaccuracies or omissions. The author reserves the right to alter or amend opinions as new conditions arise. Readers are strongly encouraged to conduct their own due diligence, verify the accuracy of information at the time of use, and seek professional advice where appropriate. This publication should not be regarded as definitive guidance, but rather as a resource to be evaluated alongside up-to-date research, independent judgment and professional counsel

Contents

Introduction

Luke buys a limited-edition sneaker for £200. A week later, he sells it online for £800 netting a £600 profit. Stories like this aren't uncommon, they're everyday examples of people spotting opportunities and turning knowledge into income.

Welcome to *The Everyday Entrepreneur*, your gateway into the profitable world of buying and selling. Whether you are looking to create a side hustle or scale into a full-time business, this guide will equip you with the strategies, insights, and tools needed to succeed.

Reselling isn't just about chasing trends, it is about recognising value, timing and opportunity. rare collectibles and trading cards to high-demand electronics and clothing, the market is vast and constantly evolving. Each section of the guide will walk you through a stage of the process, starting with how to source products, then moving on to marketing, closing sales and, if you fancy it, expanding your operation.

Flipping products for profit isn't new. But with the internet, has exploded, making reselling accessible to anyone with the drive to learn. By purchasing this guide, you have taken that first step so congrats. Today's marketplaces are just a few clicks away, offering global opportunities at your fingertips. Whether you're a complete beginner or already familiar with the process, reading this guide will help sharpen your approach and expand your earning potential.

One standout example of this accessibility is the rise of sneaker reselling. What began as a niche for collectors or '**sneakerheads**' has evolved into a multi-billion-pound industry. In 2023 the sneaker reselling alone generated an estimated £9 billion in revenue. Sneakers and their recent surge in popularity serves as a great example of how items that were once purely functional have evolved into symbols of identity, status and style. Celebrities such as music icon Drake now has his own sneaker line with

1

Nike, Nocta. Drake even owns a pair of solid gold Air Jordan 10's worth an estimated £1.5 million, highlighting the industry's pop culture significance.

Crafting your path to profit can't be done with a one-size-fits-all solution, you must be versatile and explore many avenues. You will navigate different industries, product releases, form client alliances and negotiate deals to expand your profit margins. From clothing and books to sports equipment, trading cards and even cars, the reselling world covers a vast array of products.

Using this guide, you can transform your interests into profitable endeavours. With this guide you'll learn how to turn your personal interests into profitable ventures.

Throughout, we will analyse numerous examples to illustrate key concepts, especially sneakers due to their recent boom in popularity. However, these examples and principles are intentionally chosen, to be easy to apply across various industries and to allow readers to realise profit across various markets. These industries can include sports equipment like golf clubs, football memorabilia, Lego, Vinyl's and retro sports jerseys, as well as trading cards, video games and fashionable items. Almost anything you can name holds the potential for profit if you know where to look, how to spot opportunities, and how to capitalise on them effectively.

These niches, thrive on scarcity, nostalgia and demand, offering just as much potential for profit when approached with the right knowledge and timing.

Before we jump into the hands-on strategies and real-world processes, it is important to start with a clear foundation. The reselling world moves fast, but success comes from understanding the core framework first. This opening chapter will give you a full overview of how the reselling model works and break down the blueprint that the rest of this guide is built on. Consider it your roadmap, something to keep referring back to as you move forward.

PART 1

Foundations

Chapter One

Blueprint

[re-sel-ling] noun

The practice of purchasing products, often in-demand or limited editions and selling them at a profit, typically as a business venture or hobby.

Why it Works

This reselling model thrives of the simple principle: ***supply and demand.*** When items are scarce or tied to personal identity, nostalgia, or social status, people are often willing to pay a premium. Those who recognise these trends and connect the right buyers with the right products stand to earn substantial profits. Thanks to modern online platforms this process is more accessible than ever, with low startup costs and flexible entry points that make it simple to get started.

Success in this field isn't about luck, it's about knowledge. Identifying trends, knowing where to source items, and understanding timing can transform a basic exchange into a profitable enterprise with repeated success. This knowledge is available to those willing to put in the time and effort to learn.

The Blueprint

Before we dive deeper here's a streamlined overview of the four key parts of the guide. Think of it as your roadmap a clear and structured path to help you succeed. Each part will be explored in detail across the following chapters, but here's the big picture to set you on the right track from the start.

Part 1 – The Basics

In this first part, we will go over the fundamentals and lay the groundwork for success. This section includes three additional chapters along with this one which help readers to understand value, how to capitalise on it, and the different places to find it.

Part 2 – Selling Process

With the fundamentals covered, you should now be ready to **flip** your first product. Part two focuses on the steps to successfully turn your newfound inventory into profit. These chapters usher you through every aspect of making a sale, ensuring your success.

This includes guidance on how to present your items effectively and choose the most suitable selling platforms. It also covers how to identify where your products specifically are likely to perform best and how to optimise your listings for maximum visibility and sales. Finally, it covers how important it is to implement smooth and efficient processes for shipping and delivery.

Part 3 – Expansion

Part three focuses on taking your reselling to the next level by scaling up and expanding into different strategies to generate income. It will dive into **economies of scale** while discussing strategies to help you grow your operations and uncover opportunities you may not have considered before.

Scaling up can involve mastering advanced techniques that differentiate you in competitive markets. This section provides two practical examples from the sneaker industry that highlight key growth opportunities. While we focus on sneakers, you will see how these tactics apply equally to electronics, collectibles, and more. These examples can be applied to broader opportunities, such as rebuilding and restoration, as well as leveraging emerging technologies like AI and bots. By exploring these specialised areas, you will gain valuable insights to refine your approach and stay ahead.

Beyond scaling, there are also simple but effective strategies to help boost your earnings or raise **capital** quickly, depending on how you plan to use it. These short-term tactics may not require much time or risk, but they can play a big role in helping you get started, stay afloat, or reinvest in bigger opportunities.

Part 4 – Beer Money

The final part is a bonus section that offers straightforward ways to generate extra income or build capital. Whether you see it as 'beer money,' supplemental earnings, or a method to build your starting capital, the focus is on low-effort strategies with relatively high returns.

The chapters cover various methods to raise funds, including guides on leveraging referrals, bank switching offers and side gigs. From family assistance to mutually beneficial exchanges with those around you, this section highlights how to make the most of the tools and connections already at your disposal, equipping you with quick, practical strategies to boost your financial standing.

Traits for Results

Financial Stability

It is of great importance to establish a stable financial base before embarking on any venture. Adequate capital is your passport to swift and confident purchases, allowing you to seize opportunities without hesitation. Methods for maintaining and raising capital are crucial and are uncovered in detail throughout this guide.

Interest and Knowledge

Let's take the golf market as a case study. You need to be knowledgeable about the products you're dealing with. If you're an avid golfer, you probably already know the value of premium golf balls like the Titleist Pro V1, renowned for their superior spin, consistent flight, and performance around the greens. These details set them apart from standard golf balls and make them highly sought after.

Specialised knowledge in a niche such as golf balls can be a game-changer. By leveraging your expertise in a specific niche, you can quickly identify undervalued items and flip them for profit. This applies not only to new product releases but also to the second-hand market, which is vast and full of overlooked items, and underappreciated gems. However, navigating such a market requires strategy. *Chapter Four* explores the second-hand market in detail. While it can feel daunting at first, it is one of the most valuable areas for finding unique and profitable items. It is especially useful for anyone starting with limited capital or looking to gain experience by flipping overlooked products with strong resale potential.

Customer Service

Closing a deal is just one part of the process. What truly sets you apart is what comes before and after. Providing seamless transactions and delivering exceptional customer service are essential for success and play a key role in securing repeat business. The way you package and deliver an item to a buyer is often overlooked but can significantly enhance their experience and leave a lasting impression. Attention to detail, clear communication and problem-solving skills show that you value their business and build trust for future transactions.

Adaptability is equally important, as every buyer and situation is unique. *Chapter Eight* breaks down the intricacies of shipping and customer care, offering strategies to ensure your buyers feel prioritised and satisfied. Exceptional service isn't just a nice addition, it is a crucial component.

Acquisition

Acquiring inventory is the cornerstone of any business, but it's only half of the equation. The key is not just getting items in the door but making sure to get the correct items. To start, you will need to build a solid strategy for finding inventory and spotting pieces that will sell for more than you paid.

There are various methods for sourcing inventory like, charity shops, clearance sales, wholesale suppliers, retailers' liquidation auctions and online platforms. Each of these channels has its own strengths and challenges, but to succeed, it's important to tap into a variety of them. *Chapter Three* delves into the primary methods, providing strategies on how to effectively navigate and make the most of each.

Product Presentation

Acquisition alone isn't enough. The way you present your inventory plays an equally important role in turning it into a saleable asset. Even the best items can go unnoticed if they're not showcased effectively. First impressions are key, and how you present your products can establish trust with potential buyers, encouraging them to make a purchase.

Chapter Five dives deep into the art of product photography. You'll learn how to take clear, high-quality photos that showcase your items in the best possible light. A well-photographed item communicates professionalism and value, while a poorly presented one might raise doubts, or lead to a missed sale.

Following that, *Chapter Six* focuses on the best platforms to showcase your inventory, giving the most popular ones a rating out of ten. Knowing where to sell is just as important as knowing what to sell. The right platform can make all the difference.

Tools of The Trade

The right tools make life easier and profits higher. Most of these can be operated conveniently through mobile apps or websites and many are free or low-cost, with some premium options available. Let us reveal the key tools that every seller should consider.

Cook Groups

Commonly found on platforms like Discord, they serve as powerful resources for anyone looking to gain an edge in their chosen niche. These groups operate as communities where members share valuable information, tips and updates on upcoming opportunities. From insider knowledge about limited releases to advanced tools for monitoring stock levels, **cook groups** can be a game-changer.

They can be private, subscription-based or sometimes public communities that focus on specific markets. These groups utilise apps, websites and specialised bots to gather and share valuable data. In *Chapter Nine,* we will delve deeper into cook groups, scrutinising their advantages, drawbacks and the strategies needed to operate successfully within them while maximising the insights they provide.

Apps

Staying informed is essential for success. Apps designed to track releases and trends can give you a competitive edge by keeping you updated on the latest opportunities. For instance, Droplist, a popular app in the sneaker and fashion niche, provides real-time updates on upcoming releases, locations (where they will **drop**), and other vital information. Similar tools are available for various industries, ensuring you stay ahead of the curve.

Staying up to date with news in your specific niches, such as football, can directly impact the products you acquire. For example, shifts in the football world could influence the demand for football boots, memorabilia or trading cards which are all within this niche. Using a mix of general news apps alongside those tailored to your specific interests can help you stay informed and spot emerging trends.

Payment Processors

A smooth payment experience builds trust with your customers. In some transactions, payment processors such as PayPal, Stripe and newer options like Cash App can be utilised to make it easy to manage transactions securely. Setting up and verifying your accounts properly is crucial, as is understanding the fees involved and finding ways to minimise them. Throughout the guide, we will analyse the advantages and potential pitfalls of various payment processors to help you make the best choice for your business.

Chapter Six also highlights a common scam involving PayPal and explains how to avoid it. It helps outlines safeguards to protect yourself from scams when using payment processors in general.

Final Advice

As you journey through the guide, take notes and be attentive to the information sprinkled throughout to enhance success. The guide is designed to provide a comprehensive understanding of each stage, equipping you with the insights and strategies to excel.

Remember, your experience is unique and subjective. With each chapter, you will gather more valuable tools and insights to craft your success.

Chapter Summary

❖ Reselling is buying products and flipping them for profit.

❖ Success comes from identifying opportunities tied to scarcity, nostalgia, or status and understanding when and where to act.

❖ Traits of Success: Financial stability, niche knowledge, adaptability and excellent customer service are your greatest tools.

❖ Use apps, cook groups and reliable payment processors to streamline operations and stay ahead of trends.

Chapter Two

Valuation

Value refers to the significance, importance, or usefulness attributed to something based on its perceived worth or merit.

The value of an item fluctuates based on factors such as **hype**, colours, condition, size availability, rarity and other variables. This chapter delves into addressing the central question: Why do some things command higher prices and are perceived as more valuable than others?

Brand and Rarity

Brand identity and rarity play a significant role in determining value. Together, they can elevate ordinary items into highly desirable ones.

Rarity indeed holds a unique attraction in all industries. The scarcity of a particular design or collaboration can transform it into a coveted gem among collectors and enthusiasts alike.

This was demonstrated in 2017 with the Supreme x Louis Vuitton collection. The collaboration brought together Supreme's iconic red box logo and Louis Vuitton's renowned logo in a limited series of products. The limited availability, paired with the cultural significance of the brands, sparked immense hype driving resale prices well beyond the original **retail** cost.

At the same time, brands are more than just names, they are symbols of legacy, quality and cultural impact. Renowned brands, especially those with iconic histories, command premium prices due to their established reputation and influence. Their products transcend functionality, becoming markers of status and aspiration.

The interplay of brand prestige and rarity also directly impacts value. Limited-edition items tied to culturally significant brands often carry a sense of exclusivity that makes them both more expensive and highly profitable for resale.

Condition

The condition of a product is akin to its life story, much like how a brand-new car retains its highest value compared to one that has been driven off the lot. Imagine purchasing a car fresh from the dealership, with zero miles on the odometer and that new car smell filling the interior. At this point, it holds its maximum resale value. However, the moment you drive that car off the lot, it becomes a used vehicle, and its value depreciates significantly.

This same principle applies across the board, brand-new or '**deadstock**' merchandise in pristine condition retain higher resale prices, reflecting their untouched quality and desirability.

Collaborations

Collaborations are the secret of the fashion industry. The magic often unfolds when brands unite with celebrities, designers or other influential figures. One person who profoundly shaped this space in recent years was the late Virgil Abloh.

According to a 2022 article by Time Magazine, Abloh's creative journey began when he became creative director at Donda, Kanye West's agency, after the two interned together at Fendi in Rome back in 2009. He later launched his first label, Pyrex Vision, where he reworked deadstock Ralph Lauren flannel shirts by printing the word 'Pyrex' and the number 23 on them, a tribute to his childhood hero, Michael Jordan. These shirts, originally costing $40, resold for as much as $550 each and helped lay the foundation for his more widely known brand, 'Off-White'.

But it was Abloh's work in sneakers that helped cement his legacy in the fashion history. In 2017, he partnered with Nike on 'The Ten', a collection that reimagined ten of their most iconic silhouettes. His deconstructed style, visible stitching and signature zip ties gave the shoes an unfinished, experimental feel that had never been seen before in a mainstream sneaker release. These designs pushed the boundaries between streetwear and high fashion, creating enormous hype and skyrocketing resale value.

This collaboration also marked a turning point in sneaker culture, showing that design-led storytelling and scarcity could turn a regular release into a collectible asset. Resellers quickly realised the potential. Prices for the ten models exploded on platforms like StockX, often reselling for four or five-times the retail price.

Abloh's relationship with Nike was rooted in passion. According to a 2020 Hypebeast article, he used to sleep with a pair of Jordan 5s at the foot of his bed. As a teen, he would send hand-sketched sneaker designs to Nike. While the brand initially passed on them, they eventually embraced his vision, leading to one of the most impactful collaborations in sneaker history.

In 2018, Abloh became the artistic director of menswear at Louis Vuitton, making him the first Black designer to hold that role and solidifying his position as a global cultural icon. His ability to merge luxury, streetwear and cultural relevance changed the game for how brands approached design and partnerships.

Virgil Abloh's legacy proves that when the right people collaborate with the right brands, people pay attention, and so does the market. For resellers, these are the moments to watch. Where there are big names, limited runs and brand synergy, there is money to be made.

Hype

Hype is the driving force behind excitement and anticipation for a product, creating a ripple effect that influences demand and ultimately impacts value. It fuels the buzz around releases or products, shaping consumer perceptions and decisions.When something generates substantial hype, demand often outpaces supply, creating a scarcity effect that drives up its resale value.

One key aspect of hype is its ability to elevate certain designs, colourways, or features. Products tied to broader fashion trends or cultural preferences often attract a wider audience, making them more desirable. For example, colour schemes on goods, like 'triple black' or 'all black' have become universally appealing due to their versatility and timeless nature, leading to higher resale prices for items with these attributes. This shows how specific product traits, amplified by hype, can significantly enhance perceived value.

In essence, hype can shape the narrative around a product, making it highly sought-after and driving up resale prices. For resellers, understanding and leveraging hype is crucial to identifying opportunities where demand will exceed supply, allowing them to maximise profits.

Social Media

The powerful force of social media has fundamentally changed how brands connect with their audiences, and influencers are at the heart of this shift. Think about it, have you ever seen your favourite content creator promote a brand or product? These partnerships between influencers and brands are incredibly effective, benefiting both parties. The influencer gets paid for promoting a product to their audience, while the brand enjoys increased visibility and, often, a direct boost in sales. This mutually beneficial relationship allows brands to reach a targeted demographic that trusts the influencer's opinion, creating a more authentic connection than traditional advertising.

In some cases, influencers move beyond brand deals and create their own ventures. One such example is Callum McGinley, known as 'Callux' on YouTube, who launched his own brand of the back of his success. We will now take a closer look at this unusual case, where an influencer's personal brand creation challenges the typical model of brand collaborations.

Callum initially rose to fame through his YouTube channel, known as Callux, where he started creating content for back in 2012. Over time, his channel has garnered a remarkable following, amassing four million subscribers. What sets Callux's story apart is his ability to leverage this substantial online presence to make a foray into sneakers. He ventured into the sneaker industry in 2020, unveiling his very own sneaker brand, Notoways, despite his content initially revolving around unrelated topics.

15

Remarkably, the brand has grown significantly, with Callux himself estimating on his YouTube channel that it was worth over £20 million as of 2023. The brand boasts a schedule of frequents drops, some of which did hold significant resale value. Callux's journey serves as a compelling case study of how the social media hype machine has not only allowed him to create his brand but attain success in the industry.

Notoways' success is a example of how hype and social media can open up lucrative opportunities for reselling and other ventures within the fashion industry. Brands like Childish, born out of the YouTube channel TGF, further exemplify this phenomenon. Their standout releases, particularly their hoodies, have gained recognition for their distinctive style and appeal, following a similar journey to Callux.

These products are highly sought-after due to their strong fan base and limited availability, creating an ideal scenario for flipping to eager buyers. Such items, with their dedicated audience and exclusivity, represent a prime opportunity to capitalise on their demand and achieve profits.

Celebrities

Similarly to Callux and his YouTube channel, celebrities hold immense influence in shaping trends. When a well-known figure is seen endorsing or using a particular product or service, it can generate significant excitement and drastically increase demand for that item. For instance, a celebrity spotted wearing a specific outfit or accessory can transform it into a must-have item almost overnight.

This phenomenon was and still is exemplified by Kanye West and his groundbreaking partnership with Adidas, which redefined how celebrity partnerships can elevate a brand's visibility and desirability. Let us explore this influential example further.

Kanye West, a renowned rap and fashion icon, partnered with Adidas in 2013 to create the Yeezy line. As soon as the prototypes appeared in public, the sneaker and fashion communities took notice. The Yeezy line gained a reputation for their unique design and it being Kanye's personal collaboration added an air of exclusivity and desirability. Prior to this

Kanye already had significant influence in the fashion world, with fans of the rapper even creating a website to follow his outfits called 'www.dresslikekanyewest.com' so that users could dissect his outfits in the earlier days of the internet.

This celebrity endorsement generated an unprecedented level of hype. Sneakerheads and fashion followers eagerly awaited each new Yeezy release and have done so up until, and even funnily enough after the parties seemingly split from each other in 2022.

Kanye's impact on fashion also extended beyond sneakers. His distinctive street wear style, often featuring oversized hoodies and distressed jeans, became a trendsetter's choice. People not only wanted Yeezy's but wanted to be West himself and started emulating his fashion choices. This again allowed for resellers to capitalise on fans of the icon by profiting off items associated with him.

Similarly to his best frenemy Virgil Abloh, Kanye West's Yeezy brand highlights how a celebrity's influence, whether through their personal brand, a collaboration, or even their unique style, can create a ripple effect across industries. This influence trends that impact the reselling market, so this knowledge can give you a serious edge and a serious chance to profit.

How to Profit

Now that you understand what creates value, it is time to use that knowledge. Value means nothing if you do not act on it. Here is how to apply what you know and turn it into results.

Disclaimer: The strategies in this section are accurate and applicable as of 2025 and can change.

Sell Where the Demand Lives

- Go where the buyers are. Platforms each serve different markets and understanding that is key.
- StockX and eBay are reliable for sneakers, electronics and collectibles.
- Depop thrives on vintage and trending fashion.
- TikTok Shop and Instagram are ideal for products with viral potential or influencer-led hype.
- Facebook Groups and Discord communities can be hotspots for niche buyers and bulk sales.
- For luxury or streetwear, Grailed is a strong choice.

Your goal is to match your product with the platform that best suits its audience. Learn how your niche behaves in these spaces and adapt your selling strategy accordingly.

 Tip: When starting out, use all available platforms and get a feel for them as a user. See how your product performs on each over time before tailoring your approach to specific platforms. With experience, you will develop intuition and start to recognise which platforms work best for your products and goals.

Get Ahead

By the time most people hear about a drop, it is usually too late to buy at retail. The real profits go to those who prepare in advance and catch news and rumours early. Being ahead of the crowd means you can buy at the best prices before hype drives resale values up.

Track upcoming releases, trends, and product hype using a variety of sources:

- Cook groups, niche blogs, Discord servers, and forums related to your niche.
- YouTube creators and influencers within your market
- Social media accounts and trend pages focused on your area of interest.
- Brand newsletters and official release calendars relevant to your niche.
- News outlets and culture websites that cover your sector.

Simply just be in the loop.

🔆 **Tip:** Use the reminders and notes apps on your phone to track releases and set dates in your calendar to stay prepared.

Time Your Sales

Not every item is a day-one flip. Some products peak in value over time as supply dries up or as cultural relevance increases.

Tools to help understand market timing include:

- Not every item sells best immediately after release. Some products increase in value over time as supply decreases or cultural relevance grows.
- Check price history on relevant platforms to see when an item's value usually peaks, whether right after release or later as demand grows.
- Look at sold and active listings on platforms like eBay to see current demand and pricing trends.
- Explore niche-specific marketplaces or forums to stay updated on market changes.
- Some items gain value due to wider cultural events, such as sports milestones or anniversaries related to celebrities or brands. Be aware of them.

Example: External events can change the value of your items. A limited-edition trading card might spike in value if the player has a breakthrough season. Tech gadgets could rise in demand if a new feature or update is announced. Just understanding that outside factors can affect products can help you decide the best time to sell for maximum return or even spot buying opportunities based on what you expect might happen.

Become a Trusted Seller

Your name matters. Repeat buyers are the backbone of a consistent business.

- Ship quickly and securely.
- Communicate clearly and professionally.
- Provide accurate product details.
- Package items carefully.
- Handle issues fairly and promptly.

By doing this, you can become the go-to person in your market. For example, as a golfer myself, if I ever want to buy, sell, swap, or trade, there are a few specific sellers on eBay I always use because they have built a reputation for being reliable and easy to work with. Be that person in whatever you do.

Final Word

The real opportunity lies in understanding what people want before they know they want it. Whether that is triggered by celebrity endorsements, scarcity, or social trends, your job is to read the landscape and move early.

Study the market. Learn your niche. Sell with purpose. That is how you turn hype into income.

Sizing and Models

Understanding the difference in sizing and models in your market is also imperative to be able to make sales. It also helps to understand the laws of supply and demand, which we will explore in the next section.

Let's continue using sneakers as our core example. When the supply of a particular sneaker in size 8 UK is high, its value decreases because it outweighs the demand. Conversely, if the supply is limited and the demand is high, prices and value will increase.

Similarly, the Tesla Cybertruck was announced in three models: a single-motor version at around £32,000, a dual-motor option at roughly £42,000 and a top-tier tri-motor model pushing £56,000. These prices were based on Tesla's 2021 pre-release estimates and reflect differences in range, speed and performance that buyers value most.

In the sneaker world, not all sizes or styles hold the same value. Just like cars and nearly every product released, limited runs, exclusive sizes or particular colourways can greatly shift resale prices within the same model. Variation drives perceived value, and as a reseller, learning to spot those shifts is where the opportunity lies.

Understanding the language of sizing is a primary skill, and it can impact your success. As an example, we will study how variations in sizing in footwear can impact decision-making within a niche.

Much like understanding the distinctions between models and features of a car brand, having a clear grasp of sizing and categorisation is crucial for navigating your market effectively. While this guide doesn't assume your niche will involve the same complexities, it demonstrates how breaking down an initially confusing system can make it accessible and highlight the importance of understanding the specific dynamics of the market you operate in.

This information pertains specifically to the UK, while sizing considerations for other countries are addressed later in the chapter. Let us delve deeper into this code:

TD - Toddler Sizes

Toddler Sizes (**TD**) are typically designed to cover children under the age of 3. These sizes range from UK1.5 to UK9.5, offering a variety of options for parents seeking stylish footwear for their little ones.

PS - Preschool Sizes

Preschool (**PS**) sizes, ranging from UK10 to UK2.5, cater to younger children and are again often sought after by parents looking to style their kids. However, entering this market requires caution, as it can be nuanced and challenging.

GS - Grade School Sizes

Grade School (**GS**) sizes, ranging from UK3 to UK6.5, cater to older children and are also popular amongst women who prefer men's or unisex shoe designs. GS sizes offer a profitable opportunity due to their lower **retail price** and competitive resale values, often aligning just below men's sizing.

W - Women's

Women's (**W**) sizes, spanning from UK3 to UK10, represent a somewhat less common range, yet they play a significant role in catering to diverse preferences. With a usual 1.5 size difference compared to men's shoes, these sizes accommodate a variety of styles and fits tailored specifically for women. While exclusive sneaker releases in women's sizes are relatively rare, they do occur.

Men's

Men's sizing is the most prevalent and widely used category in the footwear, typically spanning from around UK7 to UK14 and beyond for those with larger feet. The majority of shoe releases fall within this size range, making it the most familiar and straightforward for both buyers and sellers. Transactions within the niche predominantly revolve around men's sizes, highlighting its central role in the industry.

Sneaker sizing has practical implications for resellers. Sizes above 12, for instance, may not be the most lucrative to resell. Why? There are fewer people with this shoe size, and as a result, there's less stock available. This means that winning these sizes can be more challenging, and when you do there's a smaller customer base to sell to.

Verdict

So, what sizes should we set our sights on?

Statistics show that Men's UK 9 and Women's UK 6 are among the most common shoe sizes. These sizes tend to sell quickly, making them a smart choice. For example, the 'Panda Dunk' in GS size 6 became a hot commodity in 2021 and 2022, reselling for more than double its retail price of £60. Its popularity was primarily among women with a size 6 rather than younger teenagers.

Men's UK 7-11 is generally a safe range to focus on. Among these sizes, 9-11 tend to have higher stock numbers, reflecting their commonality. Common sizes are ideal because the demand is high, and there are plenty of potential buyers.

When it comes to GS sizes, they can be promising, but anything lower than a UK size 1 is unlikely to sell. Most resellers target women with smaller feet in the GS category, not older children. While some parents do buy sneakers for their children, it's a smaller market.

That is not to say there isn't a market for smaller or larger sizes. There certainly is, but these niches are more challenging and carry additional risks. They require careful consideration and strategy. On the other hand, rarer sizes can bring higher profits due to scarcity. It is about weighing the trade-offs and making informed decisions based on the market you operate in. Understanding your audience and anticipating demand will help you maximise success.

To conclude, we have broken down key sizing in sneakers considerations and how they impact resale value. While this section focused on footwear sizing, the principle of understanding product variations applies across all markets. Doing your due diligence and knowing the details of your niche is essential to avoid costly mistakes and make informed decisions. If you take one thing away from this chapter, it is this: know the market you operate in like the back of your hand so you cannot be blindsided.

Though this sizing guide focuses on footwear, the principles apply across all markets. To fully grasp what drives value, you also need to understand supply and demand because this means knowing how availability and consumer interest affect pricing and sales.

Let us now explore these fundamental market forces and how they can shape your opportunities as a reseller.

Understanding Supply and Demand

The foundation of pricing dynamics rests on the timeless principle of supply and demand. We have explored the concept of value and how it translates into demand, driven by various factors that influence what people desire. This principle is the heartbeat of the business world, dictating price fluctuations and explaining why some products reach staggering prices while others remain more accessible.

Imagine you are at a concert featuring a world-famous artist. The venue has a limited number of seats, and thousands of fans are eager to attend. Tickets for this concert are hot commodities, and everyone wants to be there.

However, the supply of tickets is fixed as it's not possible to suddenly create more seats in the arena. Now, think about how this situation affects ticket prices. With a high demand and a fixed supply, tickets become scarce. As a result, people are willing to pay a premium to secure their spot at the concert. Some might even pay well above the original ticket price just to be part of the experience.

The same fundamental principles of supply and demand apply across the board, particularly with newly released products. When a product first hits the market, it usually has a limited amount available for purchase. This limited supply, combined with strong demand and the underlying factors that drive perceived value, sets the stage for increased resale prices.

When supply is low and demand is high, prices naturally rise. Understanding this relationship is crucial for setting effective pricing strategies and making informed decisions. The inverse is also true; when demand is weak and supply saturates the market, products become readily available and lose their resale value, resulting in unsatisfactory returns. Avoiding such situations is essential for maximising profitability and mitigating risks.

Those who grasp these dynamics can capitalise on them, leveraging their knowledge to flip products at a premium. An instance of this occurred during the release of the PS5 in 2020, where resellers took advantage of a unique market situation to generate significant profits.

PS5 Launch

In the latter part of 2020, the gaming world was set ablaze with anticipation as Sony unveiled the much-awaited successor to the popular PlayStation 4 (PS4) – the PlayStation 5 (PS5). This launch marked a significant moment in the gaming industry, coming seven years after the debut of the PS4 back in November 2013.

However, the release of the PS5 also happened during the upheavals of a global pandemic, adding a unique layer of complexity to its arrival. With a release date of November 2020, the console release coincided with lockdowns and restrictions which kept people in doors.

As the world grappled with the challenges posed by the pandemic, the gaming community eagerly awaited the next-generation console, setting the stage for a release that would be unlike any other.

Demand Factors

In a landscape dominated by the PlayStation 4's success, the release of the PlayStation 5 in late 2020 generated unprecedented anticipation. Building on the legacy of its predecessor, the PS5 marked a leap in gaming technology. Boasting cutting edge graphics, exclusive titles and enhanced performance, the console became the focal point of the gaming community's excitement.

The hype around the PS5 was driven by its exclusivity. Sony revealed a strong line-up of games that could only be played on the new console. Limited information before launch and clever marketing built up even more excitement and demand.

The prospect of a revolutionary gaming console offered more than entertainment. It gave people a way to escape and stay connected during lockdown. As the release neared, the mix of new features, exclusive titles and shared hype made it even harder to get and even more desirable. This created a scarcity that heightened the desirability and resale value of the PS5.

Microchip Shortages

At the core of the PS5's supply issues were the global shortage of microchips between 2020 - 2022. Microchips, essential for the operation of gaming consoles and virtually all modern electronic devices, became a rare commodity during the pandemic. Several key factors contributed to this shortage:

- **Pandemic-Related Delays:** The global pandemic disrupted supply chains across industries. Many manufacturing plants, particularly those in key regions like China and Taiwan, had to reduce or halt production due to COVID-19 safety measures such as social distancing and shutdowns. These regions were critical for the production of microchips at the time, and their slowdown created a ripple effect in the global supply chain.
- **Geopolitical Tensions:** The strained political relationship between the U.S. and China at the time exacerbated the microchip shortage. Trade disputes and export restrictions on critical components further delayed the supply of microchips to manufacturers like Sony. With Taiwan being a leading hub for microchip production, the delicate balance of supply was thrown off, further complicating the availability of key components needed for the PS5.

- **Competing Demand:** The pandemic's impact was not limited to gaming consoles. The sudden increase in demand for electronics due to the rise of remote work, online learning, and home entertainment created a competitive environment for microchip procurement. Companies in other industries, such as the automotive and telecommunications sectors, were also vying for the limited chip supplies, intensifying the bottleneck for PS5 production.

Manufacturing

In addition to the microchip shortage, the global pandemic imposed additional challenges on Sony's production processes. With many manufacturing plants operating at reduced capacity, the entire production pipeline of the PS5 was slowed. Safety protocols in factories, reduced workforce availability and logistical issues made it difficult for Sony to distribute the PS5 in adequate quantities and limited how many consoles could be produced and shipped.

The limited supply of the PS5 also had ripple effects across the broader gaming console market. Unable to secure a PS5, many consumers turned to alternative products, such as the Xbox Series X and the Nintendo Switch, both of which faced supply challenges, albeit to a lesser extent. The pandemic-induced shift to online sales, combined with the microchip shortage, meant that all gaming consoles were in high demand and limited supply during this period.

The aforementioned shift to online retail due to COVID-19 restrictions further complicated matters. Retailers, accustomed to large in-store launches for major products, had to pivot to online sales. This shift mirrored the dynamics of sneaker drops, where scarcity and online-only releases had long been the norm. For resellers with experience in online raffles and bot technology, this shift presented an opportunity to capitalise on the limited supply.

The Reselling Frenzy

The combination of supply shortages and high demand created ideal conditions for resellers, particularly those already experienced in flipping products. The shift to online-only sales gave resellers an advantage over the general public, and their familiarity with online drops, membership in cook groups, and proficiency in using selling platforms allowed them to capitalise on the situation, outpacing regular consumers and maximising profits.

With retail prices set at around £500, the resale value of the console soared to over £1,000 past at their peak on the secondary market during the height of the frenzy.

Results from reselling can vary significantly based on market conditions, product availability, and individual effort. My earnings and the earnings of others may differ from yours and these figures are not guaranteed or typical.

Consumers, eager to get their hands on the latest gaming console, faced a difficult choice: wait months for a **restock** or pay inflated prices on the resale market. This scarcity fuelled a significant supply and demand imbalance, driving up resale prices and fostering widespread frustration among gamers.

Bot Technology

The PS5's release created a unique opportunity, as all the factors discussed converged to force the PS5 to primarily release online. This marked the first time a major gaming console launch had been restricted to mostly online sales, further intensifying the reselling frenzy as buyers had to compete in virtual queues for a chance to purchase. Many retailers were also unprepared for the challenges of facilitating fair and successful online drops, quickly discovering the impact of bot technology the hard way.

Many existing bots were modified and optimised to target the PS5 on major retail sites. These automated tools are specifically designed to rapidly complete checkouts and gave users a significant advantage in securing stock before regular consumers even had a chance. Bot technology is explored in more detail in *Chapter Eleven*.

As retailers released PS5 stock online during events like Black Friday, those familiar with bots were primed to take advantage. The bot technology worked as effectively for gaming consoles as other online drops. This gave bot users a significant edge over traditional consumers, many of whom were unfamiliar with the use of bots or the dynamics of an online drop and the speed required to secure such high-demand products, especially parents trying to buy for Christmas presents or casual consumers unaccustomed to the nuances of online drops.

Bots are a major issue in the sneaker and streetwear market, but retailers have become more adept at countering them. Measures such as address locks, one-per-user limits and other anti-**botting** strategies have long been implemented to deter, slow down or prevent their use. Without these safeguards, it became even easier for resellers to buy up large quantities of consoles, exploiting the lack of preventative measures.

Bots enabled some users to secure large portions of PS5 stock in mere seconds. Some bot users successfully secured ten or more consoles per release. A reseller who could manage to secure ten consoles could earn upwards of £3,000 in profit within a single drop.

Those without bots could also profit during this time, though on a smaller scale. By manually tracking restocks and being active in cook groups for insider tips, they could still secure one or two units per drop. Even with manual efforts, resellers could make around £300-£500 in profit per console, netting a healthy return by flipping two consoles at a time.

This lucrative opportunity persisted until the supply shortage eased by late 2022, eventually levelling out by early 2023.

This convergence of factors—pandemic-induced supply chain issues, a forced shift to online sales, the strategic use of bots by resellers, increased demand due to lockdowns, and effective marketing, created a reselling phenomenon where the PS5 became not just a sought-after gaming console but a massively profitable commodity in the resale market.

Understanding Sony's Pricing Strategy

As evidenced by the example of the PS5, where the resale price nearly doubles the retail price upon release, one might suggest that Sony should increase their retail prices.

Why do Sony not sell at 'resell prices?'

- **Consumer Backlash:** Implementing excessively high retail prices could provoke consumer backlash and tarnish Sony's brand reputation. Such pricing strategies might be perceived as exploitative or unfair by customers, resulting in negative publicity and diminished trust in the brand.

- **Resale Market Impact:** Higher retail prices might not necessarily eliminate resale activity. Instead, they could incentivise resellers to charge even higher prices, further exacerbating the affordability issue for many consumers. If they charged as much as the resellers, the resellers would then simply charge more if the demand was there , as it was for the PlayStation.

- **Long-Term Strategy:** Pricing decisions are likely guided by long-term considerations rather than short-term profit maximisation. Maintaining a balance between affordability, accessibility, and brand equity is done to sustain customer loyalty and market leadership over time.

- **Market Competition:** The PlayStation console competes with others that offer similar products at various price points. Setting excessively high retail prices could give competitors an advantage in attracting price-conscious consumers.

This analysis aims to provide insights into why retailers like Sony choose to price as they do, as well as the potential drawbacks that could arise if they were to deviate from this established pricing strategy.

Key lesson: When supply is forced online and demand soars, resellers with bot tech or simply sharp awareness can flip products for double what they paid, almost overnight.

Chapter Summary

❖ Exploring the various elements that contribute to the perceived worth of an item, including condition, demand, and brand recognition.

❖ Understanding and acknowledging how celebrities and influencers have become central figures in today's social media-driven landscape, and why their impact should not be overlooked.

❖ Recognising the significance of different sizes and models when assessing value.

❖ Using the PS5 as an example to demonstrate how an understanding of supply and demand can lead to profitable opportunities for those who grasp the concept.

Chapter Three

Sourcing

Finding the right approach and the right place to purchase your products is the initial stride towards establishing a successful operation.

In this chapter, we will cover various methods of sourcing profitable products. We will begin by exploring the broader supply chain of businesses, then narrow our focus to specific areas and opportunities where you can look to gain an advantage.

Supply Chain

Retailers and brands play a pivotal role in shaping the resell market as discussed previously. Decisions made by brands and retailers, such as producing limited releases or collaborating with influential figures, can directly impact the supply available.

To begin, let us clarify some terms and provide context to help you understand the nuances of the generic supply chain.

Manufacturer: A manufacturer is responsible for producing the good. They handle the design, material sourcing, and assembly of the final product. They create it from scratch, ensuring quality and branding are consistent with their brand image.

Wholesaler: Wholesalers purchase in bulk from manufacturers and sell to retailers, acting as intermediaries in the distribution process. Wholesalers benefit from economies of scale and typically offer products at lower prices than retailers.

Retailer: A retailer is a business that sells products directly to consumers. Retailers usually purchase from wholesalers and offer them to customers in physical stores or online. They act as distribution channels, providing accessibility to a wide range of products. Unlike manufacturers, retailers do not produce themselves, they simply sell to consumers.

Big brands can exemplify a unique case where they function as all three: manufacturer, wholesaler, and retailer.

New Balance controls the design, production and sales of their items, overseeing every step from creation to final assembly, functioning as both manufacturer and retailer. They also operate as wholesalers, selling in bulk and supplying their products to various retailers. This ensures their products reach a broad customer base. In addition to manufacturing and wholesaling, New Balance also sell directly to consumers through their own retail channels. This includes their branded stores and online platforms, where they can offer a wider selection of products and exclusive releases. It's crucial to understand that some brands often operate as more than one type of entity.

The prices at each stage of the supply chain differ due to the roles and costs involved:

- **Manufacturer Prices:** The cost of production includes materials, labour and manufacturing overheads. Manufacturers sell their products at a lower price to wholesalers or directly to retailers.
- **Wholesale Prices:** Wholesalers buy in bulk at discounted rates and then sell to retailers at a markup, though still at prices lower than retail. This helps cover their operational costs and generate profit.
- **Retailer Prices:** Retailers add another layer of markup to cover their expenses, such as store operations, marketing, and staff salaries. This results in the highest price point for the consumer.

For example, if you win some New Balance merchandise in an alternative retailer's raffle (more on raffles later), New Balance remains the manufacturer because they designed, produced and branded the product. The retailer's role in this case is simply to distribute or sell the item, they do not make or brand it.

However, this clear distinction between manufacturer and retailer does not always hold. In some industries, such as supermarkets, retailers can also act as manufacturers by producing and selling their own branded products alongside those from other manufacturers.

New Balance can again provide a useful example of how these roles can overlap. They may simply be the manufacturer when their products are sold by other retailers, like in the raffle scenario. But they can also act as both manufacturer and retailer when they sell directly to customers through their own stores or online platforms.

In short, depending on the context, a company might be only a manufacturer, only a wholesaler or only a retailer, or even all at the same time. Understanding this is important because it affects how products move through the supply chain and who controls what at each stage - from the initial concept and production to the final release and delivery to consumers.

Next, we will examine the supply chain of fitness equipment during the pandemic as a case study. This will help illustrate the complex progression and the network of players involved in a real-world example.

Fitness Equipment in the Pandemic

During the COVID-19 pandemic, the fitness industry experienced a significant transformation, particularly in the demand for home fitness equipment. With the closure of gyms and fitness centres due to lockdown measures, many individuals sought alternatives to maintain their exercise routines at home. This shift led to a surge in fitness equipment purchases, with adjustable dumbbells emerging as one of the most sought-after items. Their popularity skyrocketed due to the widespread need for compact, versatile workout solutions. Unlike traditional dumbbell racks, adjustable dumbbells offered the convenience of multiple weight options in a space-saving design, making them ideal for home use.

Understanding the supply chain of adjustable dumbbells during the pandemic provides valuable insight into how resellers can identify and capitalise on market inefficiencies. As demand surged, traditional retail supply chains struggled to keep up, leading to widespread stock shortages and price inflation. This created an opportunity for resellers to step in and profit by selling dumbbells at a premium.

A similar trend emerged with Peloton bikes during lockdown. One business, Trade My Spin, recognised both the soaring demand and the untapped supply from individuals who had purchased Pelotons but no longer used them. Instead of reselling them through existing marketplaces, the company built its own platform, purchasing used Pelotons directly from private sellers and selling them at a significant markup. This real-life case highlights the importance of understanding supply chains, sourcing strategies, and market dynamics.

Let us explore a hypothetical yet realistic supply chain for adjustable dumbbells in Covid, delving into the various stages from raw materials to the secondary market, and examining how each step contributes to the overall process.

Part 1: Raw Materials to Manufacturers

At the core of the supply chain for adjustable dumbbells are the raw materials suppliers, who provide essential materials such as steel, cast iron, rubber, and plastic. These materials are sourced from different regions across the globe, forming the foundation for the production of the dumbbells.

Once sourced, these materials are transported to manufacturing facilities where the production process begins.

Part 2: The Middlemen

After production, the adjustable dumbbells enter the distribution phase, where they are transported from manufacturing plants to warehouses and retailers. Distributors manage the flow of goods, ensuring that they are available in various retail outlets.

Retailers then receive the dumbbells and mark them up for sale, creating a price point that reflects the manufacturing costs and the retail price. This is sometimes set by the manufacturer. Big-box retailers and specialised fitness stores are key players in this distribution chain, often negotiating wholesale prices with manufacturers to secure inventory.

After that, they sell the adjustable dumbbells at a higher price to consumers. The mark-up from wholesale to retail enables manufacturers to recoup production costs and earn profits, while retailers generate revenue by selling at retail prices.

Part 3: The Resale Market

Next comes the resale market. 2020 in particular is interesting due to the pandemic, where adjustable dumbbells quickly sold out across many retailers due to the surge in demand. This shortage pushed many consumers to turn to the resale market. Much like the chaos surrounding PS5 restocks, resellers took advantage of this trend, armed with better sourcing information and access to stock, which allowed them to secure large quantities of these in-demand dumbbells and flip them for a significant profit.

Retailers, quick to recognise the shift in consumer behaviour, followed suit by increasing prices. What was once a £100-£150 set of adjustable dumbbells saw its retail price rise to £200-£300 as demand far outstripped supply. The scarcity created a perfect storm for resellers, who at the time were able to acquire stock and sell it at prices sometimes exceeding £500, depending on the brand, weight and model. This price increase didn't only come from resellers as retailers also upped their prices.

By capitalising on the supply chain gaps and the urgent demand for home fitness equipment, resellers were able to step in and fill a crucial void. This demonstrates the core concept of this chapter: with better sourcing information or stronger connections, we can unlock significant profit opportunities. The ability to acquire in-demand stock and sell it at a premium is where the real money is made.

Part 4: Understanding the Relationships

Retailers purchase adjustable dumbbells from manufacturers at wholesale prices, allowing them to make a profit from the markup to consumers. The manufacturer benefits from bulk orders, while the retailer profits from selling directly to consumers at a higher price point.

However, as seen with adjustable dumbbells, during periods of stock shortages or high demand, resellers can emerge as a key player in the supply chain. By sourcing dumbbells from retailers or second-hand markets, resellers can create their own market for the product, selling directly to consumers at a premium.

In this case, the reseller may not be part of the primary supply chain, but their presence ensures that the product reaches consumers who are willing to pay more for an in-demand item.

Part 5: Finances

Let us break down a hypothetical example to understand the financial dynamics involved in the adjustable dumbbell supply chain. These numbers are for illustrative purposes, meant to explain the dynamics of the chain and how everyone can profit.

1. Manufacturer Stage

- Total Units Produced: 10,000
- Total Production Cost: £600,000
- Cost Per Unit: £60
- Wholesale Price (to retailers): £120

Profit Calculation:

Revenue: 10,000 × £120 = £1,200,000

Profit: £1,200,000 - £600,000 = £600,000

Profit Per Unit: £60

2. Retailer Stage

- Retail Price: £200
- Units Purchased: 10,000
- Total Purchase Cost: £1,200,000

Profit Calculation:

Revenue: 10,000 × £200 = £2,000,000

Profit: £2,000,000 - £1,200,000 = £800,000

Profit Per Unit: £80

3. Reseller Stage

Purchase Price (from retailer): £200

Resell Price (on secondary market): £350

Units Purchased: 5

Profit Calculation:

Revenue: 5 × £350 = £1,750

Cost: 5 × £200 = £1,000

Profit: £1,750 - £1,000 = **£750**

Profit Per Unit: £150

4. Comparison

Stakeholder	Cost	Sell Price	Profit
Manufacturer	£60	£120	£60
Retailer	£120	£200	£80
Reseller	£200	£350	£150

5. Who Wins?

All stakeholders in this example 'win':

- Raw material suppliers earn from providing the necessary materials.
- Manufacturers profit from mass production and wholesale sales.
- Retailers generate revenue through the sale of the products at marked-up prices.
- Resellers capitalise on scarcity to sell at a premium in the secondary market.
- Consumers get access to the desired product, though often at a higher price.

6. Why This Matters

If you understand how the supply chain works, you can spot where money is being made, and more importantly, when to step in.

Every product goes through stages. Manufacturers make it. Retailers buy in bulk and sell it at a profit. When resellers are aware of an upcoming release, a demand spike, or stock drying up, they can take advantage by being faster and more flexible than big businesses. This is where your edge comes in.

For example, if you know what a product costs to make, what shops are charging and what it is reselling for, you can spot profit margins straight away. You will know when something is underpriced, when demand is about to take off, or when it is worth holding stock for a price jump.

Resellers often make more per item than big retailers, but they obviously do not make as much overall because they are working with smaller quantities. Retailers benefit from economies of scale-the more they buy the cheaper each unit gets. Resellers do not get those discounts, but they can still win by moving quicker, buying at the right time and understanding what creates value in the market.

Knowing how the supply chain works means you are not guessing. You know what a fair price looks like, when to buy in, how to price your listings and when to hold or sell. It gives you a clearer view of how the whole market functions, instead of just copying what others are doing.

If you want to compete with people who have more money, more stock and more experience, you need better timing, better judgement and better information. Understanding how pricing works at each stage gives you exactly that.

Retail Releases

Building on our new understanding of the supply chain, we will now go through the two primary strategies retailers use to release sought-after products.

Drops: Limited-Quantity Releases

A drop is a highly anticipated product release where a specific item becomes available for purchase at a predetermined time, often in restricted quantities. Here's how a drop typically unfolds:

- **Announcement:** Brands or retailers announce the release date and time.
- **Online Frenzy:** At the designated release time, buyers flock to various online platforms to secure before stocks sell out.
- **Sellout and Aftermath:** Due to overwhelming demand, popular drops sell out within minutes, and sometimes even seconds, pushing many unsuccessful buyers toward resale markets.

Example: A major brand announces a collaboration with a popular rapper, launching a limited-edition clothing line. The release is staggered over a few days across various retailers, with the largest stock dropping at 8 AM on a Saturday on website A.

As the release time nears, thousands of hopeful buyers prepare by logging into multiple devices, refreshing web pages, and preloading payment details on A. Some retailers use mobile apps instead of or alongside websites, which can alter the buying experience. In-app releases often require users to be signed in beforehand, sometimes with extra verification steps, while website-based drops rely more on speed and luck.

When the drop begins, the surge in traffic slows websites, causing loading errors and even crashes. Many buyers frantically try to add the item to their carts, only to find it sold out within moments.

Meanwhile, those using automated bots gain a significant advantage as these tools instantly detect stock, add items to carts in milliseconds, and complete the checkout process faster than any manual buyer could. This leaves many frustrated and empty-handed, forcing them to turn to resale platforms where prices have already climbed.

As bot usage has become more widespread, retailers have adapted. Many now favour a more structured and fair approach to high-demand releases: raffles. Let us explore how they work.

Raffles: A Game of Chance

Raffles employ a lottery-based mechanism where participants enter a draw for the opportunity to purchase a specific item. Raffles aim to level the playing field, as success isn't solely determined by speed or availability.

Here's how raffles function:

- **Entry Submission:** Participants provide details such as name, email, and size via online platforms or in-store to enter the raffle.
- **Random Selection:** Once the entry period closes, winners are randomly chosen. Those selected are given the chance to purchase the item, sometimes with the payment processed automatically.
- **Limited Odds:** Raffles feature lower odds of winning per entry the more entries there are, enhancing the exclusivity.

Example: A prestigious luxury watch brand is about to release a limited-edition timepiece to commemorate a significant milestone in its history. This watch, with only five thousand units being produced globally, has generated immense buzz within the watch-collecting community and beyond. Anticipation builds as the brand announces the release date, and it quickly becomes clear that demand will far outstrip supply.

The brand decides to release the watch through a raffle system. To participate, potential buyers are required to submit their details, typically including their full name, email address and specifically wrist size for watches - via the official website. The submission period is always clearly defined and participants rush to enter their information within the allotted time, each hoping for a chance to secure one of the exclusive timepieces.

Once the submission window closes, the brand conducts a random selection process. Winners are notified directly via email or app notification, and each fortunate participant is given a limited time to complete their purchase. In some cases, raffles automatically process the payment upon selection, charging the winner and shipping the watch directly to them. If the winner fails to finalise the transaction within the given window, or if there is an issue with payment, the watch is usually offered to the next randomly selected participant.

Although they may have to wait for delivery, winners can take comfort in knowing they secured one of the rare pieces at its retail price. As anticipated, many individuals weren't selected in the raffle. For them, the only remaining option to acquire the watch is through secondary markets, where we know prices can quickly escalate.

The raffle system allows the brand to maintain fairness, offering equal chances for all buyers and reducing the advantage of bots or faster internet connections. It helps to avoid the chaos and frustration that often accompanies traditional drop methods, where websites frequently crash under high demand.

While we used watches as an example, the rules and structure of raffles described here are very much standard across most raffles for high-demand products.

Prepaid and Non-Prepaid

A notable distinction in raffles is how entry fees are handled. Some raffles require prepaid entries, where the full purchase amount is charged or held as a pending transaction at the time of entry. If the participant isn't selected, the funds are released back, but they remain pending until the draw concludes. This adds a layer of financial commitment to the process, as entrants temporarily tie up their money for the chance to secure the item.

On the other hand, some raffles do not require prepayment but instead demand participants to be actively engaged during specific entry windows. These windows can vary widely—some raffles remain open for several days or weeks (the most common format), while highly exclusive releases may offer as narrow as a two-minute window at a predetermined time, announced in advance. This mixed approach blends elements of both raffles and drops, requiring quick action without immediate financial commitment.

Understanding the differences between prepaid and non-prepaid raffles is crucial, especially when multiple retailers are hosting raffles at the same time. Here's a simple breakdown to clarify the distinction:

Prepaid Raffles:

- **Fund Availability:** Requires immediate payment upon participation.
- **Pending Transaction:** Entry fee is held in a pending transaction until raffle results are announced.
- **Refund on Loss:** If not chosen as a winner, the entry fee is refunded.
- **Financial Commitment:** Adds a layer of financial commitment to participating.

Non-Prepaid Raffles:

- **Entry Window:** Participants provide details within a specific time frame.
- **Payment on Win:** Entry fee is deducted only if chosen as a winner.

Understanding the Differences

Understanding the distinctions between sourcing strategies like raffles and drops is crucial for success.

Each method comes with its own set of challenges and opportunities. Here's a quick summary of the similarities and differences to make it absolutely clear:

- **Difficulty Level:** Drops require quick reflexes and rapid purchasing skills due to high demand, while raffles introduce an element of chance, offering a fairer opportunity for all participants.
- **Flexibility:** Raffles provide more flexibility, as participants don't need to be online at a specific time: they simply need to enter during a designated period. Drops are usually at a certain time and can be a rush.
- **Multiple Platforms:** Both drops and raffles are used across various platforms, including official brand websites, retailer apps and exclusive outlets.

By understanding these distinctions, buyers can tailor their approach to maximise their chances of **copping.**

Shock Drops

Although uncommon, shock drops also exist. They are unexpected releases with no prior announcement, designed to catch consumers off guard and allow minimal time to prepare. They usually occur days before or after scheduled releases or at completely random times.

Motivations from retailers range from clearing excess stock to generating hype. While rare, it's important to be ready for them. In today's market, bots have become a nuisance for both buyers and retailers, and shock drops often act as a countermeasure to level the playing field. Their unpredictable nature makes them difficult to anticipate, so staying alert is key.

Maximising Success

Follow the pointers below to maximise your success in retailer releases, whether through raffles or drops.

1. **Join Cook Groups:** Cook groups in your niche, provide essential notifications of sudden releases Being part of these groups keeps you informed and prepared.
2. **Adequate Capital:** Ensure you have sufficient funds readily available. Multiple releases can occur, demanding quick action to secure desirables.
3. **Network and Collaborate**: Building a network of like minds can boost your success during surprise drops. Collaborating with others allows you to share insights and resources, improving your chances.
4. **Timing and Persistence:** Be persistent and don't be discouraged by initial failures. Releases can be highly competitive, and sometimes it takes several attempts to secure what you are looking for.
5. **Stay Informed:** Research and analyse previous releases to identify patterns and predict future opportunities. Stay informed through news, brand announcements, newsletters, and industry influencers to catch upcoming shock drops and trends.
6. **Optimise Your Setup:** Ensure your internet connection is fast and stable and use multiple devices or browsers to increase your chances during releases. Pre-fill payment and shipping information to speed up the checkout process.
7. **Utilise Automation Tools:** Consider using bots or automation software to increase speed and efficiency during high-demand

drops. This can give you an edge in securing limited items before they sell out.

Alternative Strategies

Retailers are not the only way to get inventory. There are many alternatives. Let's look at them below.

Second Hand

Second-hand sourcing offers another valuable avenue. Many platforms host thriving second-hand markets, featuring a wide range of items, from gently used to brand new, and even custom creations. This method can be especially advantageous during quieter periods when major retail releases are delayed, or the market slows.

Second-hand sourcing involves acquiring items online or in person, whether new or used and then reselling them for a profit. This strategy helps resellers to maintain a steady inventory and capitalise on opportunities even when retail channels are inactive. It's often recommended for those starting out or less informed, as it provides access to a broader variety of items. Additionally, it allows resellers to discover unique or rare products that might not be available through standard retail releases.

eBay is a popular second-hand platform but unlike many other platforms, eBay offers a unique bidding option where sellers can list items without a set 'buy now' price, allowing them to go to bid and be sold to the highest bidder. This feature holds importance to resellers, as it opens opportunities for profit generation. Being vigilant and actively participating in bids to secure items for resale can lead to substantial profit margins.

Effectively implementing this method on eBay involves diligent searching for auctions. through keywords such as big brands or specific models Some auctions start at 99p, presenting an excellent opportunity to capitalise on undervalued items.

This approach thrives especially for various clothing items, for example hoodies and jumpers from popular brands. By staying proactive, resellers can maximise their success in second-hand sourcing on eBay.

Additionally, it's worth noting that this method is not exclusive to bidding and can work on all online trading platforms. Buying items outright through 'buy now' options is also viable, albeit requiring more vigilant scouting as lower priced items tend to sell quickly. Nevertheless, it's worth exploring both avenues to diversify sourcing strategies and boost opportunities for profit.

 Tip: When participating in the second-hand market, particularly in auction-style bidding, set alarms or reminders for auction end times. It is often possible to win bids by placing your offer just before the auction expires. This strategy, known as 'sniping,' can give you an edge in securing desirable items at competitive prices.

Chapter Four is specifically dedicated to delving deeper into the second-hand market due to its large opportunities, offering insights on how to navigate and maximise potential profits within this sector.

Bulk Buying

Bulk buying is a strategy employed by many seasoned resellers. It involves purchasing a large quantity of product in one go, often a mix of both new and second-hand. The allure of bulk buying lies in its potential to provide resellers with an influx of cash, especially if they've accumulated excess stock over time. It's an opportunity to strike advantageous deals, whether it's acquiring a collection of vintage gems or securing a batch of the latest releases. It can be applied across all of the alternative strategies and allows sellers to benefit from economies of scale. Chapter Nine breaks down bulk buying into further detail.

Auction Houses

Auction houses can be an excellent source for second-hand inventory, particularly for those seeking valuable, rare, or bulk items. Auctions can range from general sales to niche events featuring high-end goods, antiques, or even liquidation stock. Unlike standard retail purchases, auctions allow you to determine the price you are willing to pay, sometimes leading to significant bargains.

Attending auction houses gives you the advantage of inspecting items in person before placing a bid. Many auction houses now operate online as well, making it possible to source inventory remotely. However, competition can be high, so it's important to set a budget and stick to it to avoid overpaying. This strategy applies across niches and is commonly seen in the housing market, where properties are regularly sold at auction.

 Tip: Research upcoming auctions in your area or niche and sign up for email alerts. Many auction houses provide online catalogues beforehand, allowing you to identify potential opportunities in advance.

Conventions

Conventions can be a goldmine for sourcing , providing a platform where enthusiasts, resellers, and collectors converge. These events offer a diverse array of products, from rare and exclusive releases to popular models at competitive prices. Unlike many other sourcing strategies, conventions allow for in-person inspection, enabling resellers to verify authenticity and condition before making a purchase. Engaging with vendors can also lead to bulk deals and discounts, which enhance profit margins. Networking with other attendees and sellers can help to provide valuable insights into trends and market tips.

This approach can be tailored to any niche, such as Pokémon card conventions, which are especially popular in the USA. Conventions in general are more prevalent in the US compared to the UK, largely due to the greater number of attendees and larger venues.

 Tip: To maximise success at conventions, arrive early and be prepared with cash, as many vendors prefer quick, hassle-free transactions. Also, consider bringing a price comparison app to ensure you are getting the best deals.

Treasure Hunting

While the second-hand market largely operates online today, charity and thrift shops remain valuable and often overlooked sources for sourcing inventory. The trend of 'thrifting' or —hunting for bargains and unique items, has surged in popularity, not only for personal use but also for resale opportunities.

Thrifting involves browsing through these stores to find hidden gems, whether it's high-quality clothing, rare collectibles, or valuable household items. Many have discovered unexpected treasures in these shops, from vintage pieces to brand-new goods donated by individuals or businesses.

Charity and thrift shops are worth exploring regularly, as their stock frequently changes, and you never know what you might come across. Even if you don't find something every visit, consistent searching can lead to significant finds over time. These stores shouldn't be underestimated as a viable sourcing option, whether you are looking to flip items for profit or simply score quality products at a bargain.

Friends and Family

Once you've gained experience, built a strong reputation on selling platforms, or feel confident in your skills, you can sell items on behalf of family members. Acting as a middleman allows you to leverage your expertise, established profile, and selling abilities to facilitate sales while earning a percentage of the profits.

Example: Jason's brother, John, upgrades to a new phone and wants to sell his old one to recoup some of the cost. Jason, who has an established and well-reviewed seller profile, offers to list and handle the sale on John's behalf.

They agree that Jason will take a 10% cut of the final price. If the phone sells for £400, Jason pockets £40 without any upfront cost or risk, simply by using his expertise to connect the item with the right buyer. John benefits from a hassle-free sale, and Jason profits as a trusted middleman.

Everything involved within this process is covered in detail throughout this guide, so you will have all the knowledge you need.

By letting those around you know that you buy and sell second-hand goods, you open up valuable opportunities. This approach is particularly useful for beginners, as it provides a way to source inventory, gain experience, and generate initial capital without making a financial investment.

Outlets

Outlets present an excellent opportunity for resellers to source high-quality products at discounted prices. These outlets often stock a variety of merchandise, including limited editions, overstock items, and last season's models. For resellers, the advantage is the ability to acquire authentic products at significantly reduced prices, allowing for higher profit margins when reselling. Regular visits to outlets can be highly beneficial, as inventory frequently changes, and new stock arrives. Resellers should pay attention to clearance sales and special promotions as they can offer even deeper discounts. When selecting for resale, focus on popular models and sizes, as these tend to sell quickly and at higher prices.

Storage Units

Although more common in the US, storage unit auctions present a unique opportunity for resellers willing to take a chance on unknown inventory. When renters fail to pay their fees, storage facilities auction off the contents to recover costs. These auctions can contain a mix of household goods, electronics, clothing, and even valuable collectibles—it is much like what you might see on the television show Storage Wars, where bidders compete to uncover hidden treasures in abandoned units.

Operating successfully in this field (yes, some people do this for a living) would require an entirely separate guide. However, it is beneficial to be aware of as many alternative sourcing strategies as possible as you never know when they might come in handy.

The key to success in storage unit auctions lies in experience and strategy. It takes a sharp eye for value and a willingness to take calculated risks. When done right, flipping storage unit contents can yield significant returns, especially if you have the ability to resell items effectively and have a broad knowledge of various niches.

As you explore these alternative sourcing methods, it is important to also understand how insider access can play a role. Sometimes employees use their position to get early or exclusive access to products before they reach the general public. This practice, known as **backdooring**, can provide a significant advantage by allowing resellers to acquire limited items early and profit from the initial scarcity. The next section will explain how backdooring works, its benefits and the ethical questions it raises.

Backdooring

The practice of backdooring has stirred up controversy, shedding light on the impact of personal connections within the industry. This happens when employees, often in big retail stores exploit their positions to gain exclusive access to limited releases before they officially hit the shelves or as soon as they do.

Employee Perks

Imagine Bill, a fictional employee at a retail store. Through backdooring, Bill manages to secure a pair of highly sought-after sneakers ahead of the public release. This gives Bill a double advantage: he can resell the sneakers for a profit, and their early availability makes them even more valuable due to the scarcity at that time. With virtually no pairs on the market yet, demand is high, and prices are at peak.

The retail price of the sneakers is £145. As an employee, Bill gets early access and might benefit from a staff discount, lowering his cost even further. Once secured, Bill lists the sneakers online for around £345, capitalising on the hype and limited supply. This nets him a profit of approximately £200 on a single pair.

Other employees with similar access might repeat this process multiple times, increasing their earnings before the official release.

How and Why Employees Backdoor

1. **Insider Advantage:** Employees get early information about upcoming releases and can access products before they hit the shelves. They often reserve items for themselves, friends, family, or resellers they're connected with before they are even available to the public.

2. **Early Profits:** By getting products early, employees can sell them at peak prices when supply is at its lowest.

3. **Minimal Risk:** If items don't sell as expected, employees can often return them, minimising financial risk. While there's always the chance an employer might disapprove of these actions, it is typically hard to prove any wrongdoing. Plus, backdooring is usually done on a small scale, making it less likely to attract serious attention.

4. **Building Relationships:** Employees often hook up friends and family with exclusive access, building trust and loyalty within their circle. This not only strengthens personal relationships but creates a sense of being part of an insider group.

In short, backdooring gives employees both financial rewards and stronger personal connections through exclusive access to sought-after items with minimal risk.

Example Explored

The release of the Trophy Room x Air Jordan 1 in February 2021 serves as a prominent example of backdooring. Trophy Room, owned by Marcus Jordan (Michael Jordan's son), had only 12,000 pairs of this highly sought-after sneaker available. However, as Complex reported, pairs started appearing on resale platforms before the official release date, sparking allegations that Marcus had sold large quantities directly to resellers at inflated prices.

If this did happen, Marcus would have profited significantly more than selling the sneakers at retail price, which are usually set by Nike for retailers. By backdooring, he was able to set his own price and make more money, thanks to the hype surrounding the release.

This case helps illustrate just how profitable backdooring can be. By moving products into the resale market early, sellers exploit scarcity to demand premium prices. For example, although the retail price was set at $190, resellers were listing pairs for over $2,000 before the public release.

The resellers probably paid a premium to the backdoorer, in this case Marcus, but both parties would still have made a profit. This insider advantage maximises earnings by taking advantage of high demand and limited supply.

The incident also highlights the ethical issues surrounding backdooring. Consumers expecting a fair chance to purchase these limited sneakers at retail prices were left disappointed, forced to turn to the resale market where prices had already surged. As Complex pointed out, this undermines trust in both the brands and retailers, creating frustration among loyal customers who feel excluded from the process.

The Trophy Room x Air Jordan 1 saga is a prime example of how backdooring can create massive financial opportunities while simultaneously raising questions about equity and integrity in the resale world. It is important to note that the information presented here is based on a report by Complex and refers to allegations rather than proven facts. These claims remain unconfirmed and are presented solely to illustrate the potential impact and controversies surrounding backdooring.

With cases like this highlighting the challenges, it is clear that addressing backdooring is no simple task. The following section will explore the difficulties involved in detecting and managing this practice within the industry.

The Challenges of Addressing Backdooring

- **Detection Difficulties:** Backdooring is usually done in secret, which makes it difficult for companies or authorities to detect and stop. Because these transactions are hidden, it takes more thorough investigations than usual to uncover them.
- **Legal Grey Area:** In the UK, backdooring generally falls into a legal grey area. It's usually against company policies and employment contracts, which can lead to disciplinary action or termination if an employee is caught. However, unless the practice involves clear fraud, theft or breaches of specific laws (like selling counterfeit goods or engaging in deceptive trading practices), it's not outright illegal.
- **Maintaining the Illusion:** Businesses can often employ tactics to maintain a façade of fairness while engaging in backdooring. For instance, companies may hold raffles or official sales events to give the appearance of equal opportunity, even though a significant portion of stock has already been allocated to insiders making it hard to detect.

Backdooring ultimately drives up prices and limits access, creating an uneven playing field that disadvantages the wider public. However, it is a practice in reselling and isn't going away anytime soon. While I'm not advocating for backdooring, it is worth considering that buying and selling products at a premium for profit isn't all that different and could be seen as unethical by some. I don't personally agree with this view, but it does raise important questions about the ethics of reselling.

At the end of the day, operating ethically is important, but you can't please everyone. Whether it's having someone on the inside or being part of cook groups, these can be valuable tools to boost your sourcing success.

Chapter Summary

❖ Understanding supply chains reveals the various people and businesses involved at different points. By identifying where price fluctuations occur, from manufacturer to wholesaler, retailer, and reseller, you can pinpoint opportunities to maximise profit.

❖ An examination of fitness equipment, particularly dumbbells, highlighting how supply chain disruptions lead to price changes. Recognising these shifts allows resellers to capitalise on demand while ensuring that each party in the chain is satisfied.

❖ How and why retailers use drops and raffles to release products, while managing to maximise success.

❖ Alternative methods like thrifting, clearance sales, and networking in niche communities offer unique ways to find undervalued inventory.

❖ Backdooring means getting insider access to products before release. While profitable, it carries ethical risks and can harm your reputation.

The Second-Hand Market

The second-hand market is a thriving marketplace where everyday shoppers, dedicated collectors, as well as entrepreneurs come together to buy, sell and trade used goods. It is important to understand most things within this market are used or worn. This results in prices usually being lower and opens the door of opportunity. The market has gained immense popularity in recent years, driven by factors like the exclusivity of certain models, nostalgia for vintage items and the potential for profits.

'Second Hand'

In essence, second-hand items have been previously owned, used, or worn and can vary in condition, style and rarity. Many sellers go beyond new releases and explore the second-hand market, which is especially useful during slow periods and offers great opportunities.

Collectors are a driving force behind the second-hand market. These admirers seek out rare and iconic models, often with a focus on vintage or retro styles that have stood the test of time.

A prime example of this trend can be seen in the resurgence of vintage sneakers. Classics models such as the Nike Air Jordan 4 have become highly-sought after, with even pre-owned versions commanding premium prices. One remarkable example is the Jordan 4 'Black Cat' sneakers. Originally released in 2006, they were re-released by Nike in 2020. Since then, they have steadily increased in value and are valued upwards of £750 as of 2025. Even used pairs of are considered a valuable find and usually sell for more than they did at retail, further re-emphasizing the lucrative market available and the potential for profit within the secondary market.

In *Chapter Three*, we explored various alternative sourcing strategies. Each of these methods provides a way to acquire profitable products through different sectors of the second-hand market. Now, we will shift our focus to operating safely, securely, and most importantly successfully within the online second-hand marketplace.

Importance Of Verification

Many platforms in the second-hand market now offer authenticity guarantees or similar protections. Vinted has followed the lead of market innovators like eBay by introducing an option for buyers to have items over £100 or in certain niches such as designer clothing verified for authenticity.

This added layer of security helps protect both buyers and sellers, eBay has offered a similar service for some time, which has likely been a key factor attributed to its success and dominance in the second-hand market. These guarantees are a unique feature in the second-hand market that, in my opinion, set these two platforms apart from the rest. This added layer of security and reliability makes them invaluable resources for anyone navigating the second-hand space, clearly distinguishing them from their competitors.

For newcomers or those without the necessary experience to spot counterfeits, utilising this service is highly recommended, as it can help avoid costly mistakes and provide peace of mind when buying high-value items.

Process

Upon receipt of the item, professionals conduct a thorough inspection to verify its authenticity against the listing details. If the item fails authentication or does not match the listing description, it is returned to the seller, and the buyer receives a full refund. If it is deemed genuine it is then shipped to the buyer.

In the rare instance of a return, the buyer sends the item back to the authenticator for re-evaluation of its condition. Once re-authenticated, the item is returned to the seller, ensuring transparency and accountability throughout the transaction process.

This system gives buyers added confidence when navigating the second-hand market. With that security in place, we will now return to the idea of assessing value, introduced back in *Chapter Two* but specifically within the second-hand space.

Second Hand Value

When assessing the value of an item in the second-hand market, refer to the key pointers from *Chapter Two* alongside the specific guidance provided below, tailored specifically for the secondary marketplace.

Condition is Key

The condition of second-hand items is undoubtedly the dominant factor influencing their market value. Understanding the differences in condition grading, which ranges from 'Deadstock' (DS) or 'New' to 'Heavily Worn' is important for any reseller. However, it's equally important to understand that used products encompass a spectrum of conditions, each with its unique impact on resale value. Here's a look at the most frequently used options:

Very Good: Items in very good condition show minimal signs of wear, such as slight surface marks or minor imperfections. They are well-maintained and retain strong resale value.

Good: Items categorised as 'good' may have more noticeable wear, including moderate scratches, scuffs or fading. Despite these signs of use, they remain fully functional and desirable, especially for budget-conscious buyers or collectors.

Decent: Items in decent condition exhibit moderate to heavy wear, such as visible scratches, scuffs or slight discolouration. While they may not command top-tier prices, they can still attract buyers looking for affordable options.

Worn: Products described as 'worn' typically show significant signs of use, including pronounced wear, fading or minor defects. They may still be functional but will appeal more to those looking for lower-cost or refurbishable options.

Heavily Worn: Items classified as 'heavily worn' have endured substantial wear and tear, potentially featuring deep scratches, extensive scuffs or visible damage. While their resale value is lower, they may still be useful for parts, restoration or buyers with even tighter budgets.

Recognising the significance of condition on resale value is essential, but it's equally crucial to understand that this impact can fluctuate based on factors like the model's rarity. For example, a heavily worn limited-edition sneaker could potentially command a higher price than a well-preserved common model. Each resale platform typically has its own condition grading system but these gradings are mostly similar across platforms.

This understanding of condition levels and their influence on the resale market is pivotal for success.

Once you have graded the condition, the next step is to benchmark price. Here's how to leverage live and historical listings.

Market Insights

Online listings in the second-hand market are valuable for determining the value of pre-owned items. Reviewing completed or sold listings allows sellers to assess actual selling prices of comparable products, providing insight into market demand and pricing trends. Advanced search filters enable users to refine searches by condition, brand and category, making it easier to find similar items for comparison. Different platforms may offer varying pricing perspectives due to differences in user demographics and buyer preferences, but this can help give a well-rounded view of an item's market value.

Pricing tools can further enhance value assessment by providing historical sales data, pricing trends and real-time market insights. For example, StockX offers a transparent marketplace to view past sales, bids and asking prices. Another example is Jungle Scout, typically used for analysing Amazon trends of new products, though it can still offer useful insights into demand and pricing for second-hand items before sourcing.

By leveraging these tools, sellers can identify fair prices, uncover undervalued opportunities and stay competitive. Platforms like StockX and Jungle Scout provide suggested prices based on recent sales, helping sellers make informed decisions instead of relying on guesswork. Futbin is a good example from the FIFA or EA FC niche, where the market is so popular and vast that a dedicated price checker was created to track the value of thousands of player cards. This shows how in any niche with enough demand, people develop tools to track value accurately.

Finding your own niche's price checker or market data tool can give you a crucial advantage in understanding true value and pricing items confidently.

However, such tools should be used as reference points rather than definitive pricing guides because they are not always tailored to your specific item or situation. For instance, an item with added value, such as a unique variation, bonus feature or bundled accessory may justify a higher price than the platform suggests. Relying on real data helps reduce guesswork and supports more accurate, confident pricing decisions.

With experience, sellers develop intuition and a deeper understanding of what items typically sell for, helping them make quicker and more accurate pricing decisions even without extensive research.

Keep in mind that the second-hand market is smaller and less regulated than new goods markets, requiring more educated estimates when determining value.

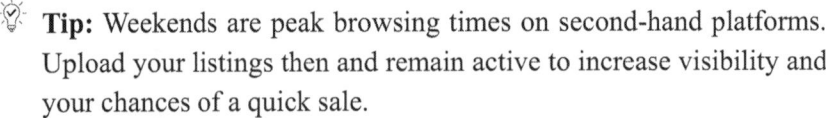 **Tip:** Weekends are peak browsing times on second-hand platforms. Upload your listings then and remain active to increase visibility and your chances of a quick sale.

Counterfeits

The battle against counterfeits is ever-present and in a market where authenticity is paramount, the unfortunate reality is the presence of counterfeits. This next section explores how to identify fakes and replicas, beginning with their origins and moving into practical methods for avoiding them market where authenticity is paramount,. Use this as your compass for identifying fakes and replicas: a skill needed for every reseller.

Origins

Counterfeit products exist across virtually every industry, from fashion and electronics to pharmaceuticals and luxury goods. The counterfeit trade thrives due to a combination of demand for cheaper alternatives, gaps in enforcement and the profitability of producing imitation goods at a fraction of the cost of authentic products.

Defining Replica and Fake

Counterfeit goods are prevalent across various industries, and distinguishing between replicas and fakes is crucial due to the differences in the imitation landscape. While both involve imitations of original products, the key distinction lies in their presentation and authorisation.

Let us establish clear definitions for these terms while noting that in many markets they are often used interchangeably, even though they are not the same. Both replicas and fakes are counterfeits, but they differ in their markets and reasons for creation.

Replica (Reps): Replicas, commonly referred to as 'reps' are usually imitations of popular apparel that aim to resemble the original. Importantly, some replicas may have been created with the consent of the original company for specific purposes, such as cost reduction or museum displays. It is common for reps to be sold with full acknowledgment of their status as imitations.

61

Fake: Fakes are unauthorized copies produced and sold with the intent to deceive consumers into believing they are purchasing genuine items. The key difference lies in the deliberate misrepresentation of the product as authentic, which can result in legal consequences for fraudulent activity.

Though both are counterfeit, confusion arises because the terms are often used interchangeably despite their important distinctions.

Why Are Counterfeits Made?

The primary motivation behind counterfeit production is simply profitability. Creating imitations of high-demand products allows counterfeit manufacturers to exploit consumer desire for premium brands without incurring the research, development, or quality control costs associated with legitimate production. Since counterfeits are often made with cheaper materials and less oversight, production costs remain low while potential profits stay high.

Another major factor is accessibility. Many legitimate brands restrict supply to maintain exclusivity or inflate prices, which drives demand in secondary markets. Counterfeiters step in to fill this demand by selling at a fraction of the cost, attracting buyers who either knowingly or unknowingly purchase counterfeits.

Many people buy counterfeit goods either knowingly, as a cheaper way to access the look and exclusivity of luxury items, or unknowingly, due to deceptive marketing and poor marketplace regulation. Counterfeits have become a popular way to engage with luxury fashion and limited releases at a fraction of the price, with high-quality replicas offering a convincing alternative to inflated retail or resale costs.

In places like Turkey, counterfeit bags, clothing and trainers are known for their quality and attract tourists searching for premium imitations, and today purchasing fakes is almost as straightforward as buying the genuine version.

Who Produces Counterfeits?

Counterfeit production is predominantly based in China, but operations exist in other countries such as Turkey, India and parts of Eastern Europe. These manufacturers range from small, unregulated workshops to large-scale factories that operate in near-identical conditions to legitimate manufacturers. Skilled workers use reverse engineering to dismantle genuine products and create detailed blueprints, ensuring the fakes closely resemble the originals.

The industry is well-organised, often involving criminal networks that coordinate production, shipping and distribution on a global scale. Counterfeits are typically smuggled through couriers and cargo shipments, sometimes disguised as generic goods to avoid detection. Next, they are sold through grey markets, street vendors, social media platforms and even major online marketplaces that fail to properly verify sellers or product.

Types of Counterfeit Goods

Counterfeits are not limited to designer clothing and luxury accessories. The market includes:

- **Electronics:** Fake smartphones, headphones, and gaming consoles that look like real brands but use inferior components.
- **Watches and jewellery:** Knockoff Rolex, Cartier and other luxury brands made with low-cost materials.
- **Cosmetics and perfumes:** Counterfeit makeup and fragrances that may contain harmful chemicals.
- **Sneakers and apparel:** Some of the most commonly counterfeited items, with brands like Nike, Adidas, and Supreme being heavily targeted.
- **Pharmaceuticals:** Fake medicines and supplements, which can pose serious health risks.
- **Automotive parts:** Inferior car parts that compromise vehicle safety.

The Impact of Counterfeit Goods

Counterfeit goods have long been a controversial topic, with arguments both for and against their existence. While they undoubtedly harm legitimate businesses and deceive some consumers, they also provide accessibility to certain products for those who knowingly purchase them. This section outlines the key impacts of counterfeits so you can form your own perspective.

Negatives

- **Financial losses for brands:** Legitimate businesses lose billions each year due to counterfeiting. This affects both large corporations and smaller independent designers who rely on originality to maintain their brand identity.
- **Job losses and economic damage:** Reduced revenue for authentic brands can lead to fewer jobs, lower wages, and decreased tax contributions that fund public services. Entire industries, such as fashion and electronics, can suffer from the counterfeit trade.
- **Safety risks:** Fake pharmaceuticals, electronics, and automotive parts can pose real dangers. Unlike genuine products that meet strict safety regulations, counterfeits often lack proper quality control, increasing the risk of malfunctions, health hazards or even life-threatening situations.
- **Exploitation and crime:** Many counterfeit factories operate under unethical conditions, sometimes involving forced labour or connections to organised crime. Profits from counterfeiting can fund illegal activities, creating a deeper societal impact beyond just fake goods.
- **Scams and uninformed buyers** Many counterfeit goods are sold deceptively, with sellers passing them off as authentic at full market value. This leads to unsuspecting buyers paying high prices for fakes, believing they are purchasing genuine products. In some cases, counterfeiters even create fake certificates of authenticity or manipulate listing photos to further deceive consumers.

Potential Benefits and Considerations

Counterfeits provides affordable access to fashion and trends. Many consumers knowingly buy high-quality replicas to engage with fashion trends they couldn't otherwise afford. Counterfeits provide a way for people to express themselves and participate in designer culture at a fraction of the price.

Ultimately, counterfeits are neither purely good nor purely bad. They exist as a complex phenomenon with various consequences. Whether you see them as a problem, or an opportunity depends on your perspective, but being aware of them and understanding both sides of the argument is crucial when navigating the second-hand market.

A Legal Perspective

Legal Disclaimer: This section is intended for informational purposes only and does not constitute legal advice. Readers should consult a qualified legal professional regarding any concerns related to intellectual property laws and counterfeit goods.

Understanding the legal intricacies surrounding replicas and fakes in the United Kingdom requires an examination of intellectual property rights, consumer protection laws, and enforcement mechanisms.

Replicas represent a spectrum of imitations that vary in quality, legality and transparency. In the UK, the sale of replicas typically involves transparency, with sellers acknowledging the imitation status of the product. However, consumers must remain vigilant, as the quality and accuracy of replicas can vary significantly and the line between replicas and fakes may blur.

Conversely, fakes are characterised by their intent to deceive consumers. These counterfeit products are sold and marketed as genuine items without the authorisation of the original manufacturer, constituting a clear violation of intellectual property rights.

In the UK, selling or distributing counterfeit goods is illegal under several laws, including the Trademarks Act 1994, the Copyright, Designs and

Patents Act 1988, and the Fraud Act 2006. Penalties can include fines and imprisonment of up to ten years, particularly for large-scale operations. While possessing counterfeit goods for personal use is generally not a criminal offence, selling them or intending to sell is punishable under Section 92 of the Trademarks Act 1994. Although prosecution for personal possession is rare, cases linked to organised crime or large-scale operations may still face legal consequences.

In addition to legal penalties, individuals involved in the sale and distribution of counterfeits may face civil liability for damages resulting from their actions. Rights holders have the option to pursue civil litigation to enforce their intellectual property rights and seek compensation for financial losses incurred as a result of counterfeit activity. Civil remedies may include damages, injunctions, and orders for the destruction of counterfeit goods.

Enforcement agencies play a critical role in combating the sale and distribution of counterfeits in the UK. The Intellectual Property Office (IPO) is responsible for administering intellectual property rights, providing guidance to rights holders, and coordinating enforcement efforts with other government agencies and law enforcement authorities. The IPO works closely with organisations such as the Police Intellectual Property Crime Unit (PIPCU), Trading Standards, and HM Revenue & Customs (HMRC) to investigate and prosecute cases of intellectual property infringement.

Ethical Selling

Integrity should always be your guiding principle. Uphold the highest standards of ethics in every transaction, ensuring that authenticity and sincerity remain at the forefront of your endeavours. Remember, your reputation is not merely built on the foundation of profits; it is deeply rooted in trust and respect. By adhering to ethical practices, you can contribute to the creation of a healthier, more transparent environment. The rules and principles below can be applied to ensuring you are a trusted seller yourself. These principles include:

- **Transparency:** Always provide complete and honest information about the product you are selling. Misleading details erode trust.
- **Authenticate**: Ensure the authenticity of your apparel to protect buyers and maintain your reputation.
- **Fair Pricing Practices:** Set fair prices based on market value, condition, and demand. Overpricing is discouraged and fairness encourages trust and repeat business.
- **Customer Service:** Maintain professionalism and respect in all customer interactions. Address inquiries and concerns promptly and strive for complete customer satisfaction.
- **Secure Transactions:** Protect customer information, maintain clear transaction records, and use secure payment methods. A secure process enhances credibility.

Embracing these ethical guidelines reflects your commitment to values beyond financial gain, establishes trust and respect. These principles create a foundation of integrity in reselling, setting an example for others to follow.

Deal Or No Deal

Navigating the second-hand market securely can be both thrilling and rewarding, especially when hunting for desirable items. The allure of this market lies in its potential to uncover hidden gems, vintage classics, limited editions and highly sought-after collectibles.

Still, along with these treasures come potential pitfalls. To ensure you are getting a great deal and safeguarding your purchases, it's crucial to approach this market with a keen eye and informed strategies. Here's twenty tips to help you do it effectively and to properly screen potential buyers and sellers.

Verification and Authenticity

1. **Ask for More Pictures:** When considering a second-hand purchase, don't rely solely on the provided images. Ask the seller for more pictures, specifically focusing on any potential defects or signs of wear. A closer look can help confirm the condition.

2. **Logo Analysis:** Examining logos is crucial in identifying counterfeits. Authentic products feature precise stitching, ensuring clean and consistent detailing and positioning. Logos should be correctly placed and aligned according to brand standards

3. **Stitching Scrutiny:** Authentic products exhibit even stitching with consistent spacing and clean finishing. Common counterfeit flaws include loose threads, uneven patterns, and sloppy craftsmanship.

4. **Verified Authentication Services:** For high-value purchases, use professional authentication services or platforms that offer authenticity guarantees.

5. **Receipts from Original Purchase:** When purchasing in the second-hand market, insist on obtaining the original purchase receipt from an authentic retailer.

6. **Authenticity Apps Limitations:** While authenticity apps can be useful, understand their limitations. They are not foolproof, and buyers should be aware that counterfeiters continuously adapt, making it possible for authenticity apps to miss nuanced details.

7. **Tags and UPC Codes:** UPC codes and SKU numbers are essential for verifying authenticity. UPC codes are globally recognised identifiers used in inventory systems to track products, while SKU numbers are unique to each item, ensuring consistency in labelling.

8. **Colourway and Model Verification:** Verify the advertised colourway and design matches authentic versions. Counterfeiters mimic unique colours, so cross-reference with reputable sources to be sure while also using your intuition

9. **Tags:** Tags alone do not guarantee authenticity. For example, StockX tags are often attached to apparel to give the appearance of legitimacy, but their presence does not confirm a product's authenticity. Counterfeit sellers frequently replicate these tags convincingly or attach genuine StockX tags to fake or replica items.

10. **Packaging Inspection:** Authentic brands maintain high packaging standards, while counterfeits often have flaws such as

incorrect box sizes or inconsistent details. Carefully examine packaging quality, as discrepancies can be a key indicator of authenticity.

Seller Assessment

1. **Effective Communication:** Establishing clear and open communication with the seller is essential. Ask questions about the item, its history, and any concerns you may have.

2. **Seller Profile Scrutiny:** A thorough examination of the seller's profile can reveal much about their trustworthiness. Pay close attention to seller ratings and reviews from previous buyers. Positive feedback is a strong indicator of reliability. Be cautious when dealing with accounts that lack history or exhibit negative reviews.

3. **Fake Reviews and Manipulation:** Some sellers manipulate ratings by using fake reviews or multiple accounts to boost their credibility. Look for verified buyer reviews, consistency in seller activity, and be cautious of sellers with only overly positive or vague feedback.

4. **Return Policies:** Ask the seller about their return policy. Sellers who are confident in their products often provide assurances and will be fine with this.

Transaction Safety

1. **Choose Trusted Platforms:** Stick to well-known and reputable online marketplaces. These platforms typically have authentication processes in place that reduce the risk of purchasing counterfeit or misrepresented products.

2. **Secure Buying:** Beware of non-standard payment methods and trust your instincts when buying online. Stick to secure, widely recognised payment options, and verify sellers especially on platforms like Instagram by checking for real human activity and watching for suspicious behaviour.

3. **Trust Your Gut:** Intuition often serves as an excellent guide. If a deal or a seller doesn't sit right with you, don't hesitate to step back and reassess.

Community Insight

1. **Be Cautious of Unbelievable Deals:** Beware of deals that appear too good to be true. While bargains can be found, unrealistically low prices are often a red flag.
2. **Stay Informed and Vigilant:** Stay updated on current market trends, common scams, and fraud tactics. The more informed you are, the better equipped you will be to identify and avoid potential pitfalls.
3. **Collaboration:** Engaging with knowledgeable communities, such as cook groups, can be invaluable. Seasoned members often have experience spotting counterfeits and can provide insights on market trends, pricing, and authenticity checks, helping you make informed purchasing decisions.

Tip: If, for any reason, doubt arises about the seller's possession of said item, a practical tip is to request a photo with the item featuring the current date and the seller's username. This additional layer of verification can be a valuable precautionary step.

By embracing these practical steps, readers can enhance their ability to distinguish authenticity. Armed with this knowledge, every transaction becomes an opportunity to master the art of authentication, ensuring a more secure and confident buying experience. Adhering to these precautions can reduce the likelihood of falling victim to scams and ensure that your transactions are secure.

Recognizing and Handling Mistakes

Mistakes happen, especially when you are a newcomer and first navigating second-hand transactions but learning from them is part of the process. If you find yourself in the unfortunate situation of suspecting you've purchased something inauthentic, fear not. Below, we will provide a guide on how to handle the situation and protect yourself.

- **Ask for a Refund (Though Unlikely):** While a refund may be unlikely, it's worth a shot. Shady sellers may resist, but it's a step worth taking if you've been duped. Those with good reviews and legit sellers will usually be open to this option.

- **Stay Informed:** Continuously educate yourself about common scams and fraud tactics in the second-hand market to stay vigilant.

- **Report to the Platform:** If the purchase occurred on a platform with an authenticity system report the issue through email or live chat. They may offer their assistance, especially if the transaction falls outside their authenticity safeguards. Selling platforms are usually good at resolving disputes fairly.

- **Write Reviews for Buyer Awareness:** Share your experience by writing reviews. By doing so, you contribute to the collective knowledge, helping others avoid the same pitfalls and fostering a more transparent market.

- **Consider Selling (with Honesty):** If allowed by the platform, consider selling, clearly stating that they are replicas. While challenging on most platforms, it might be a way to recoup some costs.

- **Learn Your Lesson:** Sometimes mistakes come at a cost. Use the steps provided earlier to avoid future blunders. Every transaction, even the less-than-ideal ones, contributes to your growth.

Remember, resilience and knowledge are your allies in transactions. The path to mastery often involves overcoming challenges, and each misstep is an opportunity for growth.

Navigating the second-hand market requires vigilance, integrity and a commitment to ethical practices. Whether you are buying or selling, maintaining transparency, verifying authenticity and prioritising customer trust are essential for long-term success. Counterfeit goods not only pose legal risks but undermine the credibility of the marketplace, making it crucial to remain informed and cautious in every transaction.

By adhering to best practices such as using reputable platforms, scrutinising product details, and avoiding deals that seem too good to be true, you can minimise risks and build a reputation as a trusted seller.

Mistakes may happen, but learning from them will make you more confident and capable in the space.

Chapter Summary

❖ Recapping the various alternative strategies for sourcing and emphasising the importance of verification when trading.

❖ Applying the methods outlined in *Chapter Two* alongside second-hand-specific valuation techniques, helping to more accurately assess an items value.

❖ Defining counterfeits, exploring their origins, and breaking down the different types and how to distinguish between them.

❖ Covering why counterfeits exist, who produces them, and the impact they have on buyers, sellers, and the market.

❖ Provided twenty key tips for trading safely online, along with how to manage mistakes.

PART 2

Making a Sale

Chapter Five

Photography

Transitioning from acquiring a product to then listing it for sale is a significant step in your venture. One of the most critical aspects of this journey is presenting your buys in the best possible light through high-quality photography. Photography plays a pivotal role in drawing potential buyers to your listings and influencing their purchasing decisions. Whether you are a seasoned photographer or a beginner, mastering these techniques set you apart.

Importance of Images

The significance of images cannot be overstated, particularly on online marketplaces. They serve as the first means of communication between you, the seller, and potential buyers. Therefore, it's essential to present your items in the best light to create a strong first impression. Successful item photos are instrumental in enhancing the appeal of your listing, with the primary picture being the most vital, serving as the first thing a potential buyer will see. Unattractive photos can harm the perception of your item's quality and authenticity, deterring buyers. Even if the item is high-quality, poor photos may suggest otherwise.

Example: When you go into your local supermarket, you don't pick the dented tin or the squashed loaf of bread, you choose the one in perfect condition. The same applies when selling online. Chances are, you won't be the only one listing that item, so standing out is key. Taking high-quality photos is one of the best ways to do that.

Thus, investing time and effort into creating visually appealing images can impact your sales and overall success on these platforms. Here are some essential photography techniques to make your listings stand out:

- **Minimalism:** Ensure your photos have a clean and uncluttered background, preferably using a solid backdrop. Remove any distracting elements to keep the focus solely on the item you are selling.
- **Perfecting Lighting:** Experiment with different lighting conditions to find the best way to showcase your product. Whether it's the softness of natural light or the ability to emphasise details with artificial light, finding your ideal lighting setup is crucial.

Tip: Avoid using the flash on your camera, as it can create harsh shadows. Instead, opt for soft, diffused lighting to ensure even illumination and minimise shadows.

- **Utilising Smartphone Cameras:** Most modern smartphone cameras offer impressive capabilities, making them suitable for product photography. There's no need to invest in an expensive camera when you can achieve excellent results with your smartphone.
- **Variety:** Provide a variety of photos showcasing different angles, details, and features to give potential buyers a comprehensive view.
- **Packaging Matters:** If your item comes with original packaging, make sure it's clean and well-presented. A neatly arranged box or packaging adds professionalism and reassures buyers about the item's condition.
- **Presentation Enhancements:** Small adjustments like stuffing a bag, shaping clothing or neatly arranging features, such as zipping up jackets or positioning straps, can significantly improve how your item appears. These refinements create a structured, polished look that helps buyers visualise the item in use.
- **Authenticity is key:** Avoid excessive editing to ensure your photos accurately represent the product.

By applying these techniques, you will create images that draw in potential buyers and effectively showcase your product.

This attention to detail also enhances the perceived value and desirability of your items. Subtle improvements can transform an ordinary photo into a polished, professional-looking image that helps buyers visualise the product in use. Taking the time to master these techniques sets you apart from competitors and builds your reputation as a trustworthy and detail-oriented seller. Ultimately, this approach to photography will help you attract more buyers, increase your sales and achieve greater success in the online marketplace.

Now that you understand how to elevate your overall presentation, it is time to focus on the image that carries the most weight, the initial photo. This image is not just another picture; it is the gateway to your listing. Because it appears in search results and previews, it deserves its own strategy and careful attention.

Primary Image

The primary image is the first image that a potential buyer will see before they click on your post or listing specifically, and as such, is very important. It is the first influence you have as a seller on potential buyers. It is the primary means of attracting attention and significantly influences a buyer's decision to click on your listing. To understand and see what makes a photo effective, it's beneficial to examine examples of good images. By doing so, you can gain insights into how to enhance the visual appeal of your listings and attract more buyers.

Scan the QR code to see examples of good listing images.

Link:
https://docs.google.com/forms/d/e/1FAIpQLSdRk0CLTvhQ9aR3qb1H4J RlWBlIMfHrM_3Svw_QaAHx8Rzh8w/viewform?usp=dialog

As you can see, the photos have the following qualities:

- **Clear backgrounds**: Some photos also include the box, which is acceptable.
- **Unedited**: The images are presented in their natural state.
- **Even lighting**: Ensuring the entire product is visible without harsh shadows.
- **Taken with a phone camera**: Demonstrating that professional equipment is not necessary for high-quality results.

The first or cover photo in an online listing is important, but we shouldn't forget, that the entire listing plays a pivotal role in attracting buyers. Most listings feature multiple photos to showcase every angle of the item. To illustrate this, we will use a real-world example by creating a product listing for the Yeezy Slide 'Granite.' Scan the next QR code to view the listing photographs.

Link:
https://docs.google.com/forms/d/e/1FAIpQLSey9uT8dV4WWNqfDwG4-G0-4muIq8Bi82Jjvip52__Cbz2KlA/viewform?usp=dialog

Title Adidas Yeezy Slide 'Granite' – UK10 Brand New in Box

Item Category Clothes, Shoes & Accessories > Men > Men's Shoes

Item Specifics

(Brand)	Yeezy
(Size)	UK 10
(Colour)	Granite
(Department)	Men
(Type)	Trainer
(Style)	Sneaker
(Condition)	New with Box

Description

Adidas Yeezy Slide 'Granite'

Size UK 10

Brand New in Box

Open To Offers

Pricing

(Format) Buy It Now

(Price) £100

(Quantity) 1

(Allow Offers) Yes

Features of an Effective Listing

Beyond just strong visuals, an effective listing includes all the supporting elements that help turn interest into a sale. While photos are crucial, the details around them, such as the title, description, item specifics and pricing, play an equally important role. To demonstrate what this looks like in practice, we will refer to a real-world example using a Yeezy Slide 'Granite' listing to highlight what makes each part effective.

- **High-Quality Photos**: The listing features three well-lit, high-quality photos that adhere to photography techniques recommended for online listings. Each photo effectively showcases the item from different angles and the packaging it comes in, allowing potential buyers to get a clear view of the product's condition and features.

- **Concise and Clear Title:** The title covers the size, condition, exact colour, and all key details without unnecessary information. It's short, clear, and attention-grabbing while including everything important.

- **Concise and Clear Description:** The description provided in the listing is concise and to the point, providing essential information about the item without overwhelming the buyer with unnecessary details.

- **Competitive Pricing:** Priced at £100 as an example, determining the right price for an item is crucial, and *Chapter Seven* will delve deeper into this topic, providing insights and strategies to help sellers price their products effectively.

- **Correct Item Specifics:** The listing includes all the correct item specifics, ensuring accuracy and clarity for potential buyers. Providing detailed item specifics such as brand, model, size, colour and condition helps buyers make informed purchasing decisions and reduces the likelihood of misunderstandings or disputes after the sale.

By following these guidelines and utilising high-quality photos, you can create a compelling listing that attracts potential buyers and increases your chances of making a sale.

Common Mistakes (and How to Fix Them)

Even with a solid understanding of how to photograph and present your item, mistakes can still occur. Below are common errors that can undermine your listing's effectiveness, along with practical solutions to help avoid or fix them:

1. Inconsistent Lighting Across Photos

Mistake: One image is well lit while another is too dark or overly shadowed, creating a jarring or unprofessional impression.

Fix: Take all photos in the same lighting environment. Use natural daylight where possible or use a consistent artificial setup to ensure visual harmony across your entire image set.

2. Overcrowded or Distracting Backgrounds

Mistake: Including clutter in the frame, such as furniture, personal items or busy patterns, which pulls attention away from the product.

Fix: Use a clean, plain background (white or neutral) or a dedicated lightbox. If none are available, hang a solid colour sheet or use a blank wall.

3. Not Highlighting Flaws or Damage

Mistake: Avoiding or hiding defects in an attempt to make the item look better, which can lead to buyer disputes or returns.

Fix: Always include clear, honest photos of any damage or wear. Transparency builds trust and sets accurate expectations and avoids issues in the future.

4. Using Filters or Heavy Editing

Mistake: Over-editing or applying filters that distort the item's true appearance.

Fix: Avoid filters and stick to natural lighting and basic adjustments for clarity. Buyers need to see what the product truly looks like.

5. Only Including One or Two Photos

Mistake: Relying on a single angle or minimal photos to represent the item.

Fix: Include multiple angles: front, back, sides, details and packaging. A minimum of three well-chosen images is a good target.

Chapter Summary

❖ Good photography is important because it helps you stand out and can lead to more sales.

❖ Going over essential techniques that ensure high-quality images for your listings.

❖ The importance of a primary image for a listing and an example with a QR code to demonstrate it.

❖ An example listing with photos, a description, and an analysis of why it's effective.

Chapter Six

Platforms

In *Chapter Three*, we covered the importance of sourcing. Once you have secured your inventory, the next step is identifying the most suitable platforms for selling it. The platform you choose can significantly affect your success, whether your goal is to maximise profits, reach a wider audience or streamline the selling process.

The marketplace is varied, with each platform offering distinct advantages, disadvantages, fee structures and user demographics. Some cater to specific audiences, while others provide broader exposure. Understanding these differences is key to making informed decisions about where to list your inventory and how best to engage with buyers, as what works for one seller may not suit another.

In this section, we explore ten of the most commonly used selling platforms, outlining their pros and cons. This overview serves as a guide to help you select the best, or combination of, platforms to maximise success. Ratings are also included to help you quickly assess each platform's overall viability.

Ratings are based on my personal experience, opinion and research.. Your experience may differ, and I am not responsible for outcomes on these platforms.

StockX

Positives

- **Large User Base:** StockX boasts a massive community of buyers and sellers, which can increase your chances of finding potential customers.
- **Price Transparency:** The platform provides historical pricing data, number of sales and other important statistics which can help you to set competitive prices on all selling platforms.
- **Authentication:** StockX authenticates items, assuring buyers of the product's legitimacy.

Negatives

- **Fees:** StockX charges high seller fees, which can eat into your profits.
- **Competition:** Due to its popularity, there's high competition from other sellers.
- **Geography**: Mostly used in the USA and not the most popular for selling in the UK.
- **Niche Specific:** Is mostly used for clothing, electronics and footwear.
- **Proof of age**: The platform is restricted to users aged eighteen and over and requires age and identity verification after a certain level of activity.
- **Limitation:** The absence of direct buyer-seller interaction might hinder negotiation.

Effective Utilisation

To most effectively use StockX, consider it a pricing tool rather than a primary selling platform, similar to how Trading 212 facilitates the sale of stocks and also provides data. While StockX is a major player in the US, where it functions more like the trading exchange it was designed to be, it's primary value in the UK lies in tracking market trends rather than selling directly.

Its market data is particularly useful for pricing, especially in niche categories. However, its focus is primarily on brand-new fashion and electronics, with no second-hand marketplace limits its versatility for resellers dealing in pre-owned goods. Additionally, its strict age policies and hefty fees may create unnecessary barriers.

Overall, StockX is a valuable tool for pricing insights but should be complemented with other selling platforms to maximise your reselling strategy.

Rating 6/10

eBay

Positives

- **Flexibility:** You have greater control over pricing and listing formats, with the option to use the auction feature, set a 'Buy Now' price, and accept offers.
- **Negotiation:** Ability for direct communication and negotiation with buyers. Offers are widely used on eBay to secure deals.
- **Authenticity Guarantee**: eBay has an authenticity guarantee on certain items over £100 to avoid the sale of counterfeits.
- **Customer Support:** Help is at hand with eBay's customer support. They're quick to respond and ready to assist via email, chat, and phone.
- **Fees:** eBay as of 2024 removed fees for sellers.

Negatives

- **Competition:** High competition, and your listings may get buried.
- **Age Verification:** eBay requires users to verify their age and identity after reaching a sales or revenue threshold, limiting access to those over eighteen. This is not necessarily a drawback but is important for under eighteen users to keep in mind.

Effective Utilisation

eBay stands as the ultimate marketplace. Its user-friendly interface, coupled with a range of options for pricing and listing details, makes it a top choice. The platform's customer service promptly addresses any issues, and the authenticity guarantee ensures a secure transaction environment for all users.

In the original draft of this guide, eBay scored a 9/10, but in October 2024, the removal of selling fees raised it to a perfect 10/10. While competition can be a drawback, readers should be able to stand out among other sellers by applying the strategies outlined in this guide.

eBay has dominated the second-hand market for decades and remains one of, if not the best, platform available.

Rating 10/10

 Tip: Exercise caution when utilising eBay's auction feature. Auctions may lead to your listings selling for less than their market value or even less than your original purchase price. Consider utilising fixed price listings or setting a reserve price to better control the selling price and protect the value of your items.

Facebook Marketplace

Positives

- **Local Sales:** Facilitates quick and straight forward sales, often involving cash transactions.
- **No Fees:** Allows you to retain the entirety of your profits, as there are no platform charges.
- **Direct:** Utilising Facebook Messenger, buyers and sellers can engage in direct, real-time communication and strike deals.
- **Facebook Groups:** The option to join focused groups on Facebook greatly enhances your reach and potential buyer discovery.

Negatives

- **Safety Concerns:** Meeting unknown individuals in person carries inherent safety risks, although such occurrences are generally rare.
- **Limited Reach:** Your audience remains predominantly local, unless you opt to provide delivery services, which can be easily arranged.
- **No Authentication:** The platform lacks built-in authentication mechanisms, underscoring the need for care in verifying authenticity.
- **Lack of Customer Support:** In cases of issues, contacting Facebook's support team can sometimes pose challenges.

Effective Utilisation

Marketplace offers valuable features, particularly the ability to connect through Facebook Groups, a unique advantage over other platforms.

At the time of writing, it lacks an integrated in-app payment system. However, users can employ direct interaction via Facebook Messenger to facilitate negotiations and then utilise alternative platforms for smoother payment and delivery processing.

Facebook can be used alongside payment platforms like PayPal, as later explored in this chapter, providing an additional means of streamlining payments. An essential inclusion in any reseller's toolkit.

Rating: 8.5/10

Instagram

Although primarily a social media platform Instagram can also be a powerful tool for selling products, offering a mix of visual appeal, some built-in shopping features, and a massive audience. Sellers can showcase items through high-quality posts, reels, and stories. With the right approach, Instagram can be a valuable tool for reaching and converting customers.

Positives

- **Visual Appeal:** Present your pieces with personalised content to captivate potential buyers visually.
- **Brand Building:** Cultivate a distinctive brand identity and a devoted following, potentially leading to increased customer loyalty and repeat business.
- **Connections:** Can help to establish meaningful relationships with customers through direct interaction.
- **Instagram Shop:** Registered businesses can now list products in an Instagram storefront.

Negatives

- **Limited Reach:** Achieving visibility on Instagram can necessitate building a substantial follower base.
- **Payment Methods:** Private sellers often need third-party payment methods, as Instagram's checkout feature is currently limited to approved businesses.
- **No Authentication:** Buyers may exhibit caution due to the absence of built-in authentication mechanisms, resulting in potential uncertainties surrounding product legitimacy.

Effective Utilisation

Instagram is a strong platform for visually driven sales, ideal for sellers aiming to build a brand and connect with buyers. Instagram Shop offers a streamlined shopping experience for registered businesses, while private sellers rely on DMs and third-party payments.

Success depends on quality content, audience engagement and trust. The platform is competitive and requires time to build a follower base. While it offers branding potential and a large audience, the lack of buyer protection and a private dedicated marketplace can make it challenging for new sellers. For those willing to grow their presence, Instagram can be an effective tool.

Rating: 6.5/10

Gumtree

Positives

- **Local Sales Advantage:** Gumtree's local focus enables you to connect with potential buyers within your immediate vicinity.
- **Fee-Free Transactions:** Enjoy the perk of no platform fees, allowing you to retain a higher portion of your sales earnings.
- **Direct Contact:** Directly engage with potential buyers through Gumtree's messaging channels, fostering a personalised and immediate interaction.

Negatives

- **Geographic Limitations:** While Gumtree excels in local transactions, its audience remains predominantly local, which may restrict your access to a broader market.
- **Safety Considerations:** Face-to-face meetings inherent to Gumtree transactions bring about safety considerations, though instances of risk are generally low.
- **Authentication Challenge:** The absence of a dedicated authenticity verification system might pose uncertainties for buyers.
- **Payment Flexibility:** Given Gumtree's lack of an integrated payment mechanism, reliance on third-party payment options is necessary.

Effective Utilisation

Gumtree offers a local marketplace for sellers seeking quick and convenient transactions, especially for in-person exchanges. It's a fee-free platform, allowing you to retain more of your profits. Be mindful of the limited reach, which is primarily local, and consider arranging deliveries to expand your market. Direct interaction with buyers and the platform's versatility for various items are the strengths of the platform. Use Gumtree strategically as a supplementary avenue alongside other platforms to enhance your exposure and capitalise on local opportunities.

Rating 6/10

 Tip: If you are going to meet a buyer through Gumtree or Marketplace, always choose a public place or meet at your home with family nearby for added safety. Negative experiences are very rare in general, and if you follow this guide's advice, such as carefully screening buyers and trusting your judgment, they are unlikely to happen.

Vinted

Positives

- **Fee-Free Selling:** Enjoy selling without incurring any platform fees as a seller on Vinted, ensuring maximum earnings.
- **Bundling Advantage:** Take advantage of Vinted's bundling feature to offer package deals and potential discounts.
- **Buyer Protection:** Vinted includes a built-in fee that guarantees buyer protection, ensuring refunds for undelivered or inauthentic items.
- **Flexible Shipping:** Choose from various shipping options, including digital labels, or normal printed ones.
- **Verification:** Vinted's new item verification service, available for designer items priced at £100 or more, provides buyers with confidence by ensuring authenticity through expert checks, offering a prepaid shipping label for the seller, and guaranteeing a full refund if the item fails verification.

Negatives

- **Limited Categories:** Focuses mainly on fashion, meaning other items may not sell as well, although it has recently expanded its platform to allow the sale of electronics as well

Effective Utilisation

Vinted is a top choice for resellers, offering fee-free transactions, an easy-to-use platform, and built-in buyer and seller protection. Sellers can also take advantage of bundling features and flexible postage options.

Originally focused on clothing, Vinted now allows the sale of beauty products, children's toys, and electronics, expanding the range of items being bought and sold. With a growing selection and a newly introduced verification system, it's clear the platform is being actively improved and developed.

Vinted was initially focused on clothing but has evolved and upgraded itself into a more complete marketplace. Initially rated as a 9/10 in the first draft, it now deserves its 10/10 score. Along with eBay, it's one of the best platforms and should be used accordingly.

Rating: 10/10

 Tip: Opting for the 24/7 InPost lockers available on Vinted can simplify your shipping process, eliminating the need for label printing and postage expenses.

Depop

Positives

- **Unique Marketplace:** Depop offers a distinct blend of social media and e-commerce, creating a personalised shopping experience.
- **Visual Storytelling:** Utilise Depop's emphasis on visuals to showcase your items with creative and engaging content.
- **Direct Interaction:** Engage directly with potential buyers through comments, messages and negotiations.
- **Community:** Depop thrives on a highly active user base, particularly in the market for second-hand designer fashion.

Negatives

- **Transaction Fees:** As of March , 2024, Depop has removed the 10% selling fee for all newly listed items in the UK. However, standard payment processing fees still apply, typically via PayPal or Depop Payments. Additionally, a marketplace fee was introduced, which will be paid by buyers on every purchase, this could impact buyer demand.

Note: Platforms like Depop and eBay have recently had to reduce or remove fees due to Vinted's explosion in popularity and its no-fee model for sellers. This is great for sellers as it creates more viable options with lower costs.

- **Authentication Gap:** Depop has some authentication partnerships for high-value designer items, including a system powered by Entrupy, an AI-driven technology that analyses materials, stitching, and other details to detect counterfeits. This service is only available for select luxury brands, meaning the vast majority of listings remain unverified, increasing the risk of counterfeit sales.

Effective Utilisation

Depop is best suited for fashion resellers who can take advantage of its trendy, social-driven marketplace. Nevertheless, the high fees and limited authentication make it less appealing for certain sellers, especially those dealing with high-value items. If using Depop, consider cross-listing on other platforms to maximise visibility and profit. Focus on high-quality images, engaging descriptions, and social interaction to stand out. While Depop isn't the best for every seller, it can still be a useful part of a broader strategy.

Rating 6/10

Etsy

Positives

- **Niche Marketplace:** Etsy is ideal for selling handmade, vintage and unique items, attracting a dedicated audience looking for one-of-a-kind products.
- **Brand Building:** The platform allows sellers to create a personalised storefront, helping to establish a strong brand identity.
- **Global Reach:** With millions of buyers worldwide, Etsy provides access to an international customer base, expanding potential sales.

Negatives

- **Transaction Fees:** Etsy charges a 6.5% fee on the total sale price, including shipping and gift wrapping. There is also a £0.16 listing fee per item. Payment processing fees vary, but in the UK they are usually 4% plus £0.20 per transaction. These fees can add up and reduce your profits.
- **Highly Competitive:** With many sellers offering similar products, standing out requires strong branding, high-quality photos, and competitive pricing.

Effective Utilisation

Given its costs, Etsy is best suited for sellers committed to building a long-term business rather than casual reselling. The same applies to platforms like Shopify, Amazon Seller Central, and dedicated business websites, which cater to businesses operating on a larger scale. Even platforms like Instagram and X (Twitter), while useful for marketing, require a strong brand presence and consistent effort to drive sales.

While it's great to aspire to grow into these platforms, they should not be used just because they're available. Instead, choose platforms that align with your current operations, business model, and goals. If you are a casual seller or focused on quick flips, a marketplace with lower fees and a built-in audience may be a better fit. However, if you aim to build a brand, scale up, and have more control over your store, then investing in platforms like Etsy or Shopify could be worthwhile.

Etsy is a strong option for serious sellers looking to build a more sustainable business, but its fees and competition make it less ideal for those looking to sell on a smaller scale.

Rating 6/10

PayPal

PayPal plays a distinct role as a transaction processing platform. It facilitates financial transactions on platforms previously mentioned such as Facebook marketplace. While it doesn't directly engage in direct selling and customer interaction, its significance cannot be overstated.

Positives

- **Middleman Facilitation:** PayPal can serve as an intermediary, ensuring secure transactions between buyers and sellers.
- **Refund Mechanism:** The platform offers a streamlined refund process in cases of disputes or issues, enhancing buyer confidence.
- **Security:** PayPal is renowned for its robust security measures, safeguarding both buyers' and sellers' financial information.

Negatives

- **Verification:** PayPal's verification procedures can lead to permanent bans for seemingly minor infractions, without the possibility of appeal.
- **Transaction Fees:** PayPal charges a standard fee of 2.9% plus £0.30 per UK transaction, which can impact profitability. Fees are higher for payments from outside the UK.
- **Potential for Scams:** While PayPal offers protection and is a safe platform, clever scammers can exploit the platforms simplicity and scam users out of their data.

Example: In this scenario, a fraudulent seller lists an item on an online marketplace. When a potential buyer expresses interest, the seller agrees to the sale but insists on payment solely through PayPal. The buyer, trusting the legitimacy of PayPal, receives what appears to be an official PayPal invoice, complete with the recognisable logo and branding. This can be through a link, text message or email. Believing it to be a standard payment process, the buyer clicks on the provided link, leading them to a convincing but fake PayPal login page.

Unknowingly, they enter their PayPal login credentials, providing the scammer access to their account. With access gained, the scammer can make unauthorised transactions on the buyer's account. Meanwhile, the seller, who potentially never even possessed the item, disappears without a trace, leaving the buyer with a compromised PayPal account and no purchased item.

This shows how scammers can exploit PayPal's reputation to deceive buyers into divulging sensitive information, such as login credentials. Although this scam has nothing to do with PayPal directly and isn't something the platform can prevent, scammers exploit its reputation to deceive buyers, making it important to stay vigilant as the consequences can be severe. A compromised PayPal account can result in unauthorised transactions, theft of personal and financial information, and potential loss of funds.

This highlights the importance of exercising caution when making online payments and using secure and reputable payment methods. Always scrutinise payment requests, especially if received via email or text, and verify their authenticity before proceeding. Vigilance is key in safeguarding against such scams and protecting oneself from financial harm.

Effective Utilisation

PayPal plays the role as a secure transaction facilitator. While not a direct selling platform, its middleman role can provide added peace of mind in your reselling exploits. Be conscious of the fees involved and take steps to prevent potential scams by following best practices. Make sure that your information is correct as the PayPal system can flag accounts for the most minor infringements. PayPal can be seamlessly integrated into your selling strategy and manage financial transactions efficiently and securely.

Rating: 8/10

Online Payment Scams

Online payment scams can result in financial loss and compromised personal information. Protect yourself from falling victim to these scams with the following tips:

- **Use Trusted Platforms:** Stick to well-known and reputable online marketplaces and payment platforms. Research the platform's security measures and user reviews before making transactions.
- **Verify Sellers:** Before making a purchase, research the seller's reputation and history of transactions. Look for reviews and ratings from other buyers to gauge their trustworthiness.
- **Monitor Your Accounts:** Regularly review your account activity and statements for any unauthorised transactions or suspicious activity. Report any discrepancies to the platform's support team immediately.
- **Beware of Requests for Direct Payment:** Be wary of sellers who insist on receiving payment through unconventional methods or outside of the platform's designated payment system. Legitimate sellers will typically accept payments through the platform's approved channels.
- **Protect Your Login Credentials:** Never provide your login credentials or personal information in response to unsolicited emails or messages. Legitimate companies will never ask for sensitive information via email or phone-especially passwords.
- **Enable Two-Factor Authentication:** Strengthen the security of your online accounts, including those on payment platforms like PayPal, by enabling two-factor authentication. This adds an extra layer of protection against unauthorised access.
- **Trust Your Instincts:** If something feels off or too good to be true, trust your instincts and proceed with caution. It's better to be safe than sorry when it comes to online transactions.

By following these tips and staying vigilant, you can reduce the risk of falling victim to online payment scams and enjoy safer transactions online. Remember, staying informed and cautious is vital to protecting yourself and your finances in the digital age.

Navigating platforms can be confusing, but each has its own strengths and weaknesses. As you gain experience, you will develop your own preferences. The best approach is to use multiple platforms to take advantage of their unique features rather than relying heavily on one. Platforms are always evolving, adding and removing features, emerging and some even fading away. So, staying informed is key to success.

The ratings and insights provided are based on my experience and feedback from others. They are subjective and may differ from your own, so use them as guidance while also forming your own opinions. I personally recommend eBay and Vinted for online selling, as they are the most convenient, easy to use, have a strong user base and charge no fees.

Chapter Summary

❖ Choosing the right platforms is a key step for success as each has its own pros and cons.

❖ PayPal functions solely as a payment processor, not a marketplace. Users should exercise extra caution when making transactions online and stay informed on how to identify and avoid potential scams.

Chapter Seven

Sales

The journey from acquiring your first item to making your initial sale involves several crucial steps. This chapter will guide you through the processes of setting competitive prices, creating attractive listings that stand out, managing the sale process, and navigating potential losses. By mastering these aspects, you will enhance your chances of a successful first sale and also build a solid foundation for future transactions.

Before we break down each step in detail, it is worth taking a moment to address those who are completely new to online selling. If you have some experience already, you may find this next section familiar. But for first-time sellers, understanding a few key basics can help avoid common mistakes and make your first sale go smoothly.

New Sellers

Eager to make her first sale, Sarah listed a designer jacket she had won in a raffle on StockX without checking the fees or fully understanding how the platform worked. She priced it based on what she thought it was worth, not using recent sales data. The jacket sold instantly. It was technically a profit, since it sold for more than she paid, but it could have gone for much more. Because of StockX's strict selling rules and high fees, Sarah ended up losing money overall and could not cancel the order without facing penalties. To help you avoid mistakes like Sarah's, use the following checklist before listing your item. It will ensure your first sale goes smoothly and without hiccups.

New Seller's Listing Checklist

- Establish the correct price point based on market research.
- Allow offers on listing to attract buyers
- Clear, high-quality photos showing the item from multiple angles.
- Accurate and detailed description including condition and any flaws.
- Correct category and subcategory for the item.
- Accurate size or dimensions where applicable.
- Clear shipping and return policy.
- Specify payment methods accepted on specific platforms.
- Double-check spelling and grammar for professionalism.

To give your listing the best chance of success, the checklist above should always be your starting point. Once that is done, it is time to create the listing and make the sale.

Your First Sale

After sourcing an item and familiarising yourself with selling platforms, it is time to create your listing and make the sale. This is where preparation meets execution. Your pricing, photos and description all need to work together to attract buyers and convert interest into a purchase. Let us walk through the steps to guide you through making that initial sale and getting comfortable with the process.

Step 1: Determining a Price

Setting the right price for your product is a skill that requires careful consideration. Use sales data and platform listings to gauge your item's market value. While there is some element of guesswork, your decision should be guided by research, trends and available data rather than guesswork alone. With experience, your ability to price effectively will improve.

Aim for a price point that is both competitive and profitable.

☀ **Tip:** Avoid undercutting, as it can lead to bricking. Bricking happens when sellers keep lowering their prices to compete, flooding the market and driving the item's value down. When everyone undercuts each other, the price drops fast, and the item becomes harder to sell at a profit. Items that lose value this way are sometimes referred to as **bricks**.

Consider the factors discussed in *Chapter Two* and *Chapter Four* to help determine an appropriate price point. Remember to review each selling platform you decide to list on, as some can incur fees that will eat into your profit margin. For some platforms, you can increase the listing price to cover the fees but be aware that this could decrease demand.

Ultimately, you can follow all the guidance available, but it is you who has to make the executive decision confidently and set the price.

Step 2: Creating a Listing

Creating a compelling and accurate listing is crucial for attracting buyers. As outlined in *Chapter Five*, high-quality photos, detailed descriptions, short and informative titles, and correct item specifics are key to making your listing effective and appealing and will help your listing stand out from the competition.

It's often beneficial to list your item on multiple platforms to maximise visibility and potential buyers. Each platform has its unique user base, so diversifying where you list can lead to more eyes on your listing.

While some platforms offer promotion options to boost visibility, it's often unnecessary if your item is in decent enough demand. Good quality listings with competitive pricing will naturally attract buyers.

Keep an eye on how your listings are performing across different platforms. If a particular listing isn't getting much attention, consider tweaking the price, description, or photos. Regularly update your listings to keep them relevant and appealing.

Step 3: Making the Sale

The time it takes to make a sale can vary from a few hours to days or even weeks. If you don't sell within a reasonable time frame, consider reassessing the price point. Once a buyer makes a purchase, the transaction typically follows these steps:

1. The buyer pays for the goods.
2. The platform holds the funds until you have shipped the item to the buyer.
3. Once the buyer receives the goods and confirms they meet their expectations, the platform may automatically deduct fees, then it will transfer the remaining funds to your bank account.
4. Your bank account receives the money from the sale.

This process follows the typical order of most online transactions. As a beginner, anticipate potential delays, such as funds being held, especially on your first sale with a new platform. Platforms often conduct more checks on your bank or transaction the first time around.

 Tip: If you receive interest in an item on a platform with high fees, consider messaging the potential buyer and suggesting a purchase on a more favourable platform. While not every buyer may agree, it's worth trying to reduce your selling costs.

This next section will guide you through key strategies and techniques to help you negotiate effectively with buyers and sellers, ensuring you secure the best possible outcomes for your sales

Negotiation

Negotiation is an essential skill in any sales-focused venture. Buyers often make offers below your expected sale price, but some offers are worth considering. The following section will help you build the understanding and confidence needed to make smart decisions. Remember, selling for slightly less than anticipated can still be worthwhile, especially considering the fluctuating nature of prices.

It allows you to:

- **Maximise Profits:** Secure better prices for your items or buy at lower costs.
- **Build Relationships:** Establish a reputation for fairness and reliability with buyers and sellers.
- **Close Deals:** Navigate differences in pricing expectations to finalise sales.

1. Preparation for Negotiation

Preparation is key to successful negotiation. Here's how to get ready:

- **Research:** Before entering a negotiation, make sure you are well informed about the topic at hand. Know the value your item has and any alternatives within the market. This information gives you leverage.
- **Set Clear Objectives:** Determine your minimum acceptable price and ideal target price. Having a clear goal helps you negotiate effectively and avoid settling for less than you are comfortable with.

2. Effective Negotiation Techniques

To negotiate successfully, consider these techniques:

- **Anchor Pricing:** Start with a higher initial price to give yourself room for negotiation. This technique allows you to adjust while still achieving a desirable outcome.
- **Build Rapport:** Establish a positive connection with the buyer or seller. People are more likely to engage in fair negotiations when they feel respected and understood.
- **Counteroffers:** When you receive a counteroffer, evaluate it carefully and respond with a counteroffer that balances your goals with the other party's expectations.
- **Effective Communication:** Use clear language, avoid slang and maintain a respectful manner even if negotiations become tense.

3. Common Negotiation Scenarios

Certain situations come up often and will begin to feel natural with time. Being familiar with these helps you stay prepared and respond effectively.

- **Offers:** If you receive an offer significantly below your asking price always respond professionally. You can either firmly reject the offer or counter with a reasonable price that still nets you a profit.
- **Bundling Deals:** Consider offering bundle deals to increase perceived value. For example, if a buyer is interested in multiple items, offering a discount for purchasing all at once can be an effective negotiation tactic.

✅ **Tip:** Bundling is also a great way to shift slower-moving items by pairing them with more desirable stock.

- **Last-Minute Haggling:** Some buyers wait until the final moment like just before payment or when meeting in person to try and knock the price down. Be ready for it and decide beforehand how flexible you are willing to be. Do not be afraid to walk away if the revised price does not work for you.
- **"Can I Pay Later?" Requests:** You may get buyers asking to reserve the item until payday or offering to split payments. Unless you know and trust them, it is best to avoid this. Always try to secure full payment upfront to reduce risk.
- **Take-It-or-Leave-It Offers:** Some buyers will send blunt messages like "£20 today or nothing" in an attempt to pressure you. These are rarely worth entertaining unless the offer already matches what you are happy with. Stand your ground and do not be afraid to pass on deals that do not suit you.

4. Closing the Deal

Once an agreement is reached, ensure a smooth closure:

- **Confirm Terms:** Clearly restate the agreed-upon terms to avoid misunderstandings. Confirm details such as price, payment method and delivery arrangements.
- **Follow Up:** After finalising the deal, follow up with the buyer or seller to confirm receipt of payment or delivery of the item. A follow-up ensures satisfaction and can pave the way for future transactions.

5. Avoiding Common Pitfalls

Be aware of these potential pitfalls:

- **Being Too Rigid:** Flexibility is key in negotiations. Sticking too rigidly to your initial terms can result in missed opportunities.
- **Over-Negotiating:** Excessive bargaining can deter buyers or sellers. Strive for a balance between achieving your goals and maintaining a positive negotiation experience.
- **Ignoring Red Flags:** Pay attention to warning signs, such as a buyer's reluctance to provide details or alternative payment methods. Avoid buyers or sellers that display these red flags like those listed in *Chapter Four,* to avoid problematic transactions.
- **Handling Losses:** Handling losses involves recognising when an item's value has dropped and adjusting your strategy accordingly. Accepting losses as learning experiences enables you to refine your strategies and improve future transactions.

Mastering negotiation requires a blend of preparation and effective communication. By understanding negotiation and applying these techniques, you can enhance your ability to close deals successfully and maximise your profitability. Remember, negotiation is a skill that improves with practice, so continue refining your approach and learning from each experience.

While strong negotiation skills can boost your sales and improve your margins, even the most skilled sellers face occasional setbacks. Challenges are natural and learning how to handle them is just as important as closing a good deal. The next section will help you navigate these hurdles and continue progressing with confidence.

Overcoming Challenges

Challenges are an inherent and, in fact, an expected part of trading online. Every seller, whether a beginner or seasoned pro, encounters hurdles along the way. These challenges can take various forms, from temporary obstacles to more persistent issues. Remember that challenges are often opportunities in disguise. Here's how to navigate and overcome common hurdles:

Slow Sales Periods

Every seller, no matter how successful, will experience slow sales periods from time to time. There might be weeks or even months when your inventory isn't moving as quickly as you'd like. During these times, remain patient and don't lose sight of your long-term goals. Here's what you can do:

- **Diversify Your Inventory:** Consider adding different types of products or expanding into related products to attract a broader audience.
- **Discount Strategically:** Offer limited-time discounts or promotions to stimulate sales without compromising your profits.
- **Reevaluate Your Pricing:** Take a fresh look at your pricing strategy and compare it to the current market trends.
- **Bite the Bullet:** Occasionally, you may find yourself in a situation where the value of a purchase plummets below what you originally paid or projected. In such cases, it's sometimes wiser to 'bite the bullet' and minimise your losses by selling at a loss. This experience can serve as a valuable lesson and help you avoid making similar mistakes in the future.

Handling Difficult Customers

Dealing with challenging customers is part and parcel of the business. They might be dissatisfied with their purchase, have unrealistic expectations, or simply be difficult to communicate with. Here's how to handle such situations:

- **High Standard:** Always address customer inquiries and concerns with courtesy and respect.
- **Effective Communication:** Listen actively to their concerns, ask clarifying questions, and provide clear and honest solutions.
- **Set Clear Policies:** Have well-defined return and exchange policies in place and communicate them clearly to customers.
- **Resolve Disputes:** If a dispute arises, try to find a mutually agreeable solution rather than escalating the situation. Platforms tend to favour the buyer, even if they are in the wrong.

Market Fluctuations

Market trends can be unpredictable. Prices can fluctuate, demand can shift, and new releases can influence the overall landscape. To navigate these fluctuations:

- **Stay Informed:** Keep a close eye on news, follow market trends, and stay updated on upcoming releases in your market.
- **Flexible Pricing:** Be willing to adjust your pricing strategy according to market demand and competition.
- **Diversify Your Portfolio:** Don't rely too heavily on a single product, niche or brand, diversify your inventory to spread risk.

Challenges, setbacks, and unexpected situations are all part of the process. But being prepared and aware of these difficulties is far better than being overwhelmed when they inevitably arise. Every successful seller has faced obstacles, and those who endure are the ones who adapt, learn, and keep moving forward. With the right mindset and strategies, you can turn even the toughest situations into opportunities for growth.

Final Thought

Your first sale is just the beginning. With each transaction, you'll gain confidence, sharpen your skills, and learn something new. Keep going. Consistency, adaptability, and a bit of hustle will take you far.

Chapter Summary

- ❖ Going over each individual step of completing your first online sale and how this will look.
- ❖ Successful negotiation involves preparation, clear objectives, effective communication and techniques like anchor pricing and bundling. Balancing flexibility with firm decision-making helps maximise profits, close deals and minimise pitfalls.
- ❖ Overcoming challenges such as slow sales periods, market fluctuations and difficult customers is key to building experience.

Chapter Eight

Shipping & Customer Service

The process continues after the sale, and what follows is equally important. This chapter delves into specific aspects of shipping and customer service, providing you with the tools and insights needed to ensure smooth transactions and build a strong brand reputation. We'll cover everything from packaging and returns to international shipping and communication strategies.

Shipping Costs and Pricing

Determining the right shipping costs is a key aspect for success. It involves striking a balance by providing competitive rates for your customers while ensuring your own expenses are covered. To achieve this balance, consider several factors in your pricing strategy:

Shipping Method: The chosen shipping method affects the cost. Different services offer varying rates and levels of compensation in case of issues. Transparency in your pricing strategy is paramount. Being upfront with your customers about shipping costs not only builds trust but also helps to manage their expectations.

Package Specifics: The weight and size of your package play a role in determining shipping costs. Heavier or bulkier packages naturally incur higher shipping fees.

Premium Shipping Options: When dealing with high-value items, opting for premium shipping options is a prudent move. For instance, Royal Mail offers:

- **First Class Signed For:** This service, priced at around £5 (subject to variations based on size and weight), provides added security, although it only offers compensation up to £50 in the case of any issues.
- **Royal Mail Special Delivery:** At approximately £10, this premium option covers shipments up to £750. While seemingly more expensive, it offers risk mitigation. Buyers often appreciate the extra care, particularly for collectibles or luxury items.

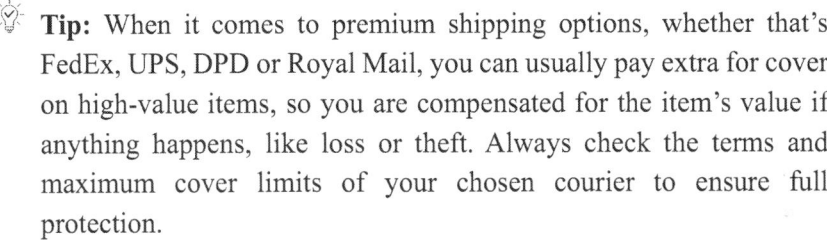 **Tip:** When it comes to premium shipping options, whether that's FedEx, UPS, DPD or Royal Mail, you can usually pay extra for cover on high-value items, so you are compensated for the item's value if anything happens, like loss or theft. Always check the terms and maximum cover limits of your chosen courier to ensure full protection.

Information above is correct as of 2024 but is subject to change. The options will still probably be the same, but price and conditions may change so stay alert and do your own due diligence. The key takeaway here is simple: do not compromise on postage costs, especially for valuables. While most items reach their destinations safely, having premium shipping options as a precautionary measure can save you from potential losses and maintain your reputation as a reliable seller.

Remember, most buyers are willing to pay a bit extra for the peace of mind that comes with secure shipping. By making informed choices in your shipping strategy, you not only protect your interests but enhance your customers confidence in your operation.

Printer: Essential or Excess?

The decision to invest in a printer in order to print shipping labels and cards yourself is one that might cross your mind. Let us delve into the pros and cons to help you make an informed choice.

Pros and Cons

Owning a printer can be convenient, but it's not always necessary, and you can always influence your buyers to choose more favourable shipping options for you if you don't have one. Here's a closer look at the pros and cons:

Pros:

- **Time-Saver**: Printing labels and other shipping-related documents at home can save you trips to the post office or courier drop-off points.
- **Platform Compatibility**: Some platforms integrate seamlessly with printers, allowing you to generate shipping labels directly.
- **Additional Uses:** Printers can be utilised for creating business cards and thank-you notes, adding a professional touch to your transactions. Alternatively, you can pay for this service separately.

Cons:

- **Cost**: Printers themselves can be costly, and the labels needed for printers also incur a cost.

Verdict

For casual and new sellers, owning a printer is not a requirement. Most modern platforms like Vinted and InPost offer digital shipping solutions using QR codes, which can be scanned at drop-off points with the courier applying the label for you. InPost lockers, in particular, are available 24/7 and are extremely convenient for sending low-value or one-off items without needing any equipment at home. Royal Mail and some other couriers even offer free label printing at the post office once postage is purchased online, meaning you can operate smoothly without a printer.

These flexible options lower the barrier to entry and remove upfront costs, allowing you to get started with minimal setup.

However, if your operation grows and you are regularly processing large volumes of sales—think hundreds of orders a month, such as running a clothing line or an established Etsy shop, then investing in a printer can significantly streamline your workflow. It allows you to print and apply labels at home, which saves time and reduces reliance on third-party services or local printing facilities. Thermal printers can be especially efficient and cost-effective long-term, as they do not require ink and typically print faster than regular inkjet printers. Prices range from £20 to £200, making it a scalable upgrade when your business reaches the point of needing it.

That said, even with a printer, you will usually still need to visit a drop-off point or arrange courier collection, depending on your shipping method. Some platforms also require physical labels to be attached before accepting packages, so having your own printer becomes more of a necessity at that level. Ultimately, your choice regarding a printer should align with your business needs and preferences. If you believe you can get by without one, you probably can, especially in the early stages. Focus first on building your sales and using the available digital shipping tools. Once volume and time-efficiency become priorities, then consider adding a printer to your setup.

 Tip: To minimise trips, choose one or two specific days each week (depending on your volume of sales) to go to a locker or a post office. Instead of making daily trips with single parcels, consolidate your packages and go once a week with multiple parcels to save time.

Now that you understand shipping costs and methods, let's turn to a crucial but often overlooked part of the process, packaging and protecting your items.

Packaging and Protection

Another cornerstone of success is ensuring that the items you send reach their new owners in the same condition they left you in. This means that packaging plays a critical role in safeguarding during transit. Let us dive deeper into the art of packaging and explore the materials and techniques that can make all the difference.

1. Choose the Right Packaging Materials

When it comes to packaging, your selection of materials is pivotal. Here are some packaging materials to consider:

- **Boxes:** Sturdy, appropriately sized boxes are the foundation of secure packaging. Make sure the product fits snugly in the box without too much extra space to prevent movement during shipping.
- **Bubble Wrap:** Bubble wrap is an excellent cushioning material. Wrapping products individually to protect them from impact and friction during transit can help to protect them.
- **Packing Peanuts:** These lightweight, cushioning fillers add an extra layer of protection within the box. They help keep the contents in place and absorb shocks during handling.
- **Tape:** High-quality packaging tape helps to seal the box securely. Ensure all seams are well-taped to prevent accidental openings. However, if your item is brand new or a collector's item, avoid applying tape directly to the box, as this could affect its value.
- **Fragile Stickers:** If your items are particularly delicate, consider adding 'fragile' stickers to alert handlers to handle the package with care although this can be excessive in certain cases.

While not all additional items are essential and may slightly increase costs, investing in enhancing your customers' experience can yield notable benefits. By providing exceptional service and going the extra mile, you can improve customer satisfaction, garner positive reviews, and build a strong reputation. These satisfied customers are more likely to return for future purchases and may even recommend you to others, ultimately contributing to long-term success and profitability.

 Tip: Keep packaging from items you've purchased. You can reuse packaging by turning it inside out, saving you money and increasing your profits. Packing peanuts and bubble wrap among other things can also be saved.

2. Labelling and Addressing

Proper labelling and addressing are essential to ensure your package arrives to its destination smoothly:

- **Clear Labels:** Use clear, legible labels for both the recipient's address and your return address. Include your contact information in case any issues arise during shipping.

3. The Unboxing Experience

While not a necessity, creating a positive unboxing experience can enhance your image and encourage positive reviews. Consider including some of these personalised touches:

- **Branding:** If you have a logo, social media presence such as an Instagram page, or other branding for your business, consider incorporating it into your packaging to create a memorable impression. This could include custom stickers, business cards or other branded elements that reflect your identity and help build recognition.
- **Thank-You Notes:** Include a small thank-you note expressing your appreciation for the purchase.
- **Extras:** Some sellers include small extras like discount codes for future purchases as a token of gratitude.

Remember, secure packaging protects your item while also leaving a lasting impression on your buyers. It demonstrates professionalism, care, and attention to detail, which can lead to positive reviews and repeat business. While packaging materials may incur some additional costs, the investment is well worth it for the safety of your valuable merchandise and the satisfaction of your customers.

Once you have this under control, you can confidently explore the opportunities and challenges of reaching a wider, international audience. The next section will guide you through the important considerations involved in shipping overseas, including tariffs, duties and other factors that can impact your global sales strategy.

International Shipping

Expanding your reach to include international shipping can be a complex move, but it comes with its share of complexities and opportunities. Here, we will explore the intricacies involved in catering to a global customer base and how to overcome potential challenges.

Tariffs and Import Duties

Tariffs and import duties are charges imposed by a country's government on imported goods. They serve multiple purposes, from protecting domestic industries to generating revenue for the government. Import duties vary widely between countries and can impact the cost for an international buyer.

Example: Let us say you are shipping a pair of sneakers worth £150 from the United Kingdom to a customer in the United States. When the sneakers arrive, the buyer may have to pay import duties, which can range anywhere from 0% to 20% depending on the product type and materials. For footwear, this is often around 10% of the declared value, so the buyer might pay about £15 in duties.

In addition to duties, the buyer may also have to pay customs processing fees or taxes applied by the courier or customs authorities. These charges vary by courier and country but are typically a fixed fee or a percentage of the value. This means the final cost the customer pays could be noticeably higher than the original price of £150.

Import duties and fees are usually paid by the buyer before the item is released for delivery. This added cost often discourages international purchases unless the product is unique or worth the extra expense. However, not all buyers are fully aware of these charges when placing an order. They might only be notified once the package reaches customs, where payment is required before delivery. This unexpected cost can lead to delays, frustration or even refusal to pay, causing the item to be returned or abandoned. These complications add friction to the transaction and often make the product less competitive compared to similar items available locally without extra fees.

For sellers, the reality is that international shipping often brings more hassle than reward, especially when the profit margin is similar to what could be made from a straightforward domestic sale. Unless the demand, pricing or product uniqueness clearly justify it, sticking to local buyers is usually the more efficient and profitable choice.

The same applies when buying from other countries, import duties and tariffs can add unexpected costs, making an item far pricier than it initially seems. These fees fluctuate due to factors like politics and economic shifts, adding uncertainty. At the time of writing in 2025, the shifting Trump tariffs were changing frequently and adding extra uncertainty, something sellers should always keep in mind when dealing with international markets.

While international shipping is a viable option, it's generally not recommended especially when starting out unless the circumstances make it truly worthwhile.

Shipping Costs

International shipping costs depend on several factors, including the weight and dimensions of the package, the shipping method chosen, and the destination country.

Accurately calculate shipping costs prior to shipping to avoid undercharging or overcharging your customers.

Example: Shipping a 500g parcel from the UK to Australia via standard international post may cost around £10 to £15, compared to approximately £2.50 to £4.00 domestically. Be mindful that shipping costs vary by location, and high international fees can easily discourage buyers since they add significantly to the total price.

 Tip: Some sellers offer 'free shipping' by building the cost into the product price. Always question why someone would ship for free, since it still costs money. While you should watch out for this as a buyer, it can also be a clever tactic to use yourself when selling.

Customs Forms and Documentation

If you do decide to ship internationally, customs forms and documentation are usually needed. These documents detail the contents of the package, its value, and other necessary information. Accurate and complete paperwork is critical to avoid customs delays or rejections. These can vary depending on what country you're shipping too.

Example: You are shipping a limited-edition comic to a collector in Germany. The customs declaration should include specific details about the comic book, such as its title, edition, and value. Incomplete or inaccurate documentation can result in customs holding the package, causing delays for you and the customer.

Shipping Insurance

Shipping insurance provides financial protection in case of loss, damage, or theft during transit. It's especially needed for high-value items. This is only recommended for items that are of high value and that would cause issues if lost.

An example of this is Royal Mail's Special Delivery Guaranteed by 1PM service. This service typically costs around £12, depending on the package's weight and size. You can upgrade the cover for an additional fee, with options up to £2500. It's important to only purchase shipping insurance that matches the value of your item. For instance, if your item is worth £200, insuring it for £2500 is unnecessary and a waste of money.

Ensure the coverage accurately reflects the item's value to avoid overspending on insurance.

Example: You are sending some rare Pokémon cards worth £1,000 to a buyer in France. By purchasing shipping insurance, you ensure that if the package is lost or damaged during international transit, you can file a claim and receive compensation to cover the cost.

Navigating the Terrain

To successfully navigate international shipping, follow these practical tips:

1. **Thoroughly Research Tariffs and Duties**: Research the import duties and tariffs of the countries you plan to ship to. Familiarise yourself with how these fees can impact you and your customers' costs.

2. **Accurate Shipping Calculations**: Use reliable shipping calculators to provide accurate shipping costs to international customers. Ensure that these costs reflect the chosen shipping method and destination.

3. **Clear and Complete Documentation**: Fill out customs forms accurately and comprehensively. Double-check that all necessary documents are included with each shipment.

4. **Insurance Considerations**: Evaluate the value of your package and decide whether shipping insurance is warranted. This decision should factor in the item's value, shipping destination, and potential risks during transit.

5. **Proactive Customer Communication**: Keep international customers informed about the shipping process, potential customs delays, and tracking details.

International shipping presents both challenges and exciting growth opportunities for your business. While it may impact your bottom line, understanding the nuances of global shipping and providing exceptional customer service can enable you to successfully expand your reach and elevate your reputation on a global scale. While it's generally discouraged due to potential cost implications, if you've thoroughly followed all the necessary steps, conducted calculations, and believe it to be worthwhile, then pursuing international shipping can be a viable option for you.

To wrap up this chapter, it is just as important to understand how to handle what comes after shipping, especially when things go wrong. Let us now look at the most common issues sellers face and how to avoid or resolve them effectively.

Handling Returns and Issues

While your goal is always to provide excellent products and smooth transactions, issues can still arise. Whether it is a return, a delay, or a complaint, being prepared for these situations is key. How you handle problems when they do occur plays a big role in shaping your reputation. This section will show you how to put yourself in the best position to avoid common pitfalls and deal with challenges effectively if they happen.

1. Clear Return Policies and Response Time

Not having clear return policies, or responding slowly to customer inquiries can cause issues. Establish clear return policies upfront and respond promptly. Use the platform's return systems to streamline the process and aim for solutions that work for both you and your customer.

2. Customer Communication

Acting rashly or aggressively when handling customer issues, can escalate problems. Be sure to communicate calmly and stay in control. Keep in touch with buyers throughout the shipping process, providing tracking details and maintaining transparency about order status.

3. Proof of Postage

Failing to keep proof of postage, can lead to difficulties resolving disputes. Always maintain evidence such as photos of postage and receipts. This proactive step helps resolve shipping issues quickly and smoothly.

4. Not Encouraging Customer Reviews

Many sellers overlook the importance of customer reviews and feedback. Encourage customers to leave reviews, and provide exceptional customer service. Positive feedback builds your reputation and helps set you apart in the marketplace.

Great customer service and reliable shipping may not be the flashiest aspects of reselling, but they are the foundation of a trustworthy and professional brand. By being thoughtful, proactive and consistently working to avoid common mistakes, you will set yourself apart and give customers every reason to come back.

Chapter Summary

❖ Determine shipping costs carefully to balance customer satisfaction and cover expenses.

❖ Owning a printer can save time, but evaluate the costs and benefits based on your platform and business needs.

❖ Secure packaging using the right materials and techniques is essential for protecting your reputation.

❖ Before venturing into international shipping, it's crucial to have an astute understanding of tariffs, costs, required documents, and insurance.

❖ Handling returns and issues professionally can lead to positive resolutions and maintain customer trust.

PART 3

Expansion

Chapter Nine

Expansion

Expansion is the moment your reselling journey can shift from a side hustle into a serious business. In this chapter, we explore the strategies and structures like cook groups, bulk buying and business incorporation that can help you to scale confidently.

Notice: If you reside outside the UK, it is crucial to conduct your own due diligence to understand the applicable laws and regulations in your country.

Expansion Strategies

Cook Groups

Cook groups are exclusive online communities for specific niches. These groups can be your secret weapon, offering insider knowledge and real-time market intelligence. They are usually found on platforms like Telegram and Discord.

Benefits

- **Alerts to Shock Drops:** Provide real-time notifications about surprise releases allowing you to be among the first to secure coveted releases.
- **Stock Numbers:** Access insider information on stock numbers, helping you make more informed buying decisions.
- **Tutorials and Guidance:** They offer a wealth of tutorials and insights, like the ones found in this guide.
- **Retailer List:** Gain access to an extensive list of retailers and websites where profitable releases are available.

- **Release Schedules:** Some provide detailed release schedules, helping you plan your purchases strategically.
- **Giveaways:** Some groups offer giveaways, providing opportunities to acquire free items. While these can add value to your inventory, they should be seen as a bonus rather than the main motivation for joining.
- **Networking:** Being a part of a group naturally fosters interaction with other sellers, helping you build a customer base and connect with individuals on a similar journey. These connections can lead to collaborations and valuable partnerships.

Where?

To join a cook group consider looking:

- **Online:** Look for articles, blog posts, and forum discussions that recommend reputable groups. Platforms like Reddit and Telegram, specifically dedicated to reselling or your niche, can be valuable resources.
- **Social media:** Follow influencers and resellers on social media platforms, as they often share insights about the cook groups they are part of, promote or recommend.
- **Word of Mouth:** Networking with other resellers can lead to invitations or recommendations for more exclusive cook groups.

Cost

The cost of joining a cook group varies widely. Some charge a monthly fee between £1 and £50, while premium groups can cost hundreds for exclusive access and advanced tools. Free groups exist, but they often lack the same insider information and support. Choosing a group that fits your budget and goals can improve your odds of success and keep you ahead of the competition. Only maintain a subscription if the group continues to provide value.

Always research a cook group before joining, especially if it charges high fees. Look for trusted reviews and avoid any group that seems vague or makes unrealistic promises. Once you are part of a group, reassess its value before each payment cycle. If it no longer meets your needs or you feel you have gained all you can from it, consider exploring other options.

Red Flags

Before joining any cook group, especially one that charges money, stay alert for the following warning signs:

- **Lack of Transparency:** If the group does not clearly state what it offers or avoids sharing proof of success or results, proceed with caution.
- **Overpromising Results:** Be wary of claims that sound too good to be true, such as 'guaranteed profits' or 'instant success with no effort.'
- **No Trial or Previews:** Most quality groups give some form of preview, screenshots, or testimonials. A total lack of insight before payment is a red flag.
- **Pushy Sales Tactics:** If the group pressures you to join quickly due to 'limited spaces' or uses countdown timers to rush decisions, take another look.
- **Anonymous or Unverifiable Admins:** If you cannot verify who runs the group or see any feedback on them, you may be putting your money at risk.
- **No Community Engagement:** A dead chat, lack of activity, or minimal interaction from admins may indicate a low-value or abandoned group.

Trust your instincts. If something feels off, walk away. There are plenty of quality, well-run groups available that provide real value for your money.

 Tip: Use cook groups and tools as part of a broader strategy. While they're invaluable resources, combining this knowledge with your own research and expertise will give you the ultimate edge.

If you become highly skilled and build an audience or following in your niche, you might consider starting your own cook group to generate extra income using your specialised knowledge. However, this can be

129

challenging and typically requires extensive experience and an established audience to be able to offer something valuable.

The more time you spend in cook groups, the more likely you are to come across members looking to offload stock in larger quantities. These moments create the perfect entry point into bulk buying, where stronger connections and quicker decisions can lead to bigger profits.

Bulk Buying

Bulk buying is a common practice in the business world where companies purchase large quantities of goods at a discounted rate. This strategy works just as well for resellers.

When applied to reselling, bulk buying can be a lucrative strategy, demanding a larger capital investment but offering the potential for significant returns. For example, this means buying a large number of products for a substantial sum. So why would people sell or buy in bulk?

Let us explore the reasons below.

- **Quick Cash Injection**: Some sellers may want to liquidate their stock for a quick cash injection. This presents an opportunity for you to buy in bulk at potentially lower prices. When sellers need to free up capital or move inventory quickly, you can swoop in and make advantageous deals.

- 💡 **Tip:** Sometimes a seller may be trying to offload stock that did not sell as expected. Be cautious and follow the steps outlined in this guide before committing to bulk purchases.

- **Cash Flow Management**: Bulk buying ensures a consistent flow of inventory, reducing the need to rely solely on retail purchases. Having a steady stream of product ready for sale allows you to maintain an active presence in the market and cater to the demands of your customer base.

- **Alternative to Retail**: Instead of exclusively buying from retailers, you can source your inventory from other sellers looking to offload stock. This approach can provide you with unique selections that might not be available through traditional retail channels.

Bulk buying can significantly enhance your activity by providing cost savings, ensuring a steady inventory and offering unique purchasing opportunities. However, it is crucial to manage your capital wisely and ensure that the goods you buy in bulk have a strong resale potential.

While bulk buying can offer big rewards, it also comes with its own risks. Here's how to navigate those challenges wisely.

Risk Management

It's vital to understand and manage the risks associated with bulk buying, such as holding inventory for extended periods, which can tie up capital and the less likely but serious threat of encountering counterfeit or replica items.

To minimise these risks, it's important to take precautionary measures and adopt a strategic approach.

The following strategies, along with those discussed in *Chapter Four* can help protect you and ensure smoother bulk purchases.

- **Diversify Your Inventory**: Avoid putting all your capital into a single model of merchandise. Instead, diversify your purchases across different models, sizes, brands and even niches. This reduces the risk of being heavily impacted if one product doesn't perform well.
- **Stay Informed:** Continuously monitor market trends and demand fluctuations. This will help you adapt your inventory and pricing strategies accordingly. Being aware of what is losing appeal can prompt you to sell them sooner rather than later.
- **Set Clear Sales Goals**: Define specific sales goals and time frames for each batch you purchase in bulk. This ensures you have a plan for moving inventory and limits the risk of holding onto stock for extended periods.
- **Have an Exit Strategy**: Be prepared with an exit strategy in case certain products don't perform as expected. This might involve

adjusting your pricing, marketing, or even considering wholesale options yourself to offload excess inventory.

What This Looks Like

Reece connects with a reliable supplier he met with through an exclusive cook group. The supplier deals in second hand smartphones and occasionally runs into cash flow problems. To free up funds quickly, he sometimes offloads stock below market value.

In one deal, the supplier needs to raise money quickly, and Reece offers to buy a batch of thirty phones at £320 each. These phones typically sell on the second-hand market for around £400. To protect both sides, they arrange the deal through a trusted middleman: an admin of the cook group where they met. The admin holds the funds, allowing Reece to verify the legitimacy and working condition of the phones upon receipt. Once the supplier ships the phones and they are confirmed to match the agreed terms, the admin releases Reece's £9,600 payment to the supplier.

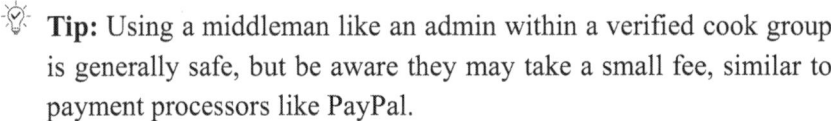 **Tip:** Using a middleman like an admin within a verified cook group is generally safe, but be aware they may take a small fee, similar to payment processors like PayPal.

Reece already has a proven system in place and is experienced with the sale of phones. He lists the phones across different platforms, uses photos he took upon delivery, and ensures each buyer covers shipping as to not eat into his profits. He only sells through platforms that charge no fees to maximise profits, and he checks every phone to reduce the risk of disputes or returns as is his process and strategy.

Reece eventually sells all thirty phones individually across multiple selling platforms over the next two months, generating £12,000 in revenue. This approach of listing each phone individually carries risks such as price changes, slowing demand and disputes that could reduce profits. Although it takes time, effort and patience to list and manage each sale, by taking on the risk, trusting himself, being patient and putting in the work, Reece benefits. After subtracting the £9,600 he paid, he nets a £2,400 profit through careful preparation and persistence.

Why the Supplier Accepts Reece's Offer

- He instantly receives a large sum of £9,600, providing quick access to much-needed cash.
- He avoids the hassle of listing, posting and selling phones one at a time.
- He eliminates all risks associated with selling phones individually, including slow sales, price drops and returns.

Everyone benefits. The supplier turns stock into quick cash without the hassle of individual sales. Reece earns a solid profit by stepping in with capital, a clear resale strategy and the patience to see it through. Buyers still receive a fully working phone at the standard market price, no different than if they had purchased directly from the original supplier.

As explained back in *Chapter Three*, this is the same model that drives large-scale retail. Wholesalers offload bulk stock for a variety of reasons, in our example to solve a cash flow issue. Retailers, or in this our example, resellers, take on the task of breaking that stock into individual sales to earn higher returns. Reece is simply applying the same principle on a smaller, more manageable scale. Most resellers can operate as small-scale retailers by using the same strategies as major stores, such as bulk buying and patient selling. This is how modern business works, and resellers can take part in it just the same.

With more capital and experience, deals like this become both more frequent and more profitable. As your resources grow, so does your ability to take on larger opportunities. This is the natural progression of expansion. Having more capital allows you to access better deals, which in turn generate more profit and create a cycle of growth.

Bulk buying opens the door to bigger opportunities, but it often requires more capital than most new resellers have available. This leads to a common challenge: how to fund larger purchases when you are just starting out or still building momentum. If your own savings are limited, one of the most practical and accessible ways to raise capital is by involving the people closest to you. That is where the support of family, friends or colleagues can come into play.

Family Utilisation

Another way to scale is by asking parents, older siblings, cousins, colleagues or friends for a loan or support to help you start or expand. This section explains how to build their trust and show them why it is worth backing you.

Note: This section is especially relevant for those who are younger, still in education, not currently earning or earning but with little to no disposable income due to other financial commitments. It outlines how you can use other people to help kick-start or expand your venture.

First Steps

Building Trust: Explain your intentions clearly and ensure it makes financial sense to them. By doing so, you build trust and establish yourself as a financially responsible individual. Assure them that you are committed to repaying any loans promptly and with interest, demonstrating your reliability.

Clear Plan: Outline exactly how you intend to use the money and how it will generate a return. Show them a breakdown of expected costs, potential profits and a timeline for repayment. The more transparent and detailed you are, the more confidence they will have in lending to you.

Incentives: Consider making it worthwhile for them by offering a percentage of the profits or a fixed interest rate on the loan. This can turn the arrangement into a mutually beneficial investment rather than just a favour. By offering a share of the profits, you create a win-win scenario. Emphasise how their investment can potentially yield substantial returns

Starting Small: If they are hesitant, start with a smaller loan to prove your ability to handle the responsibility. Successfully repaying a small amount on time can build trust and open the door for larger investments in the future.

These strategies work in real situations, beyond the theoretical level. To show how family support can play out in practice, here is a simple example of how a small loan, clear communication and trust can lead to a win for both sides.

Jack and Jane

Meet Jack, a sixteen-year-old college student who spent his Christmas money on an Xbox and some new football boots. With no money left but a desire to flip console games, he turns to his older sister, Jane, who is nineteen and has her first job.

Jack asks Jane for a loan of £100 to bulk buy 10 Xbox games on marketplace he believes he can resell for profit. She agrees, recognising the potential for profit due to Jack outlining his plan. Jack makes a smart move, buying and selling all the games for £150 total.

After accounting for platform and postage fees of 10%, Jack gives Jane back her £100, plus an extra £10 as a token of appreciation for her support. This equates to a 10% return on her investment. Jane is satisfied with the outcome and now trusts Jack to repay her for future opportunities.

Jack, armed with his initial success, has made £25 in profit. Though modest, this initial profit is a stepping stone. Repeating the process can lead to consistent, compounding gains. Both parties have benefited, and Jack now has a foothold and some experience reselling. This example illustrates how involving family members can be a mutually beneficial arrangement.

Financial Responsibility

As your ventures grow, maintaining meticulous financial records and following tax laws becomes essential. Accurate documentation is not only crucial for fulfilling tax obligations but for complying with the specific financial regulations that govern selling and reselling activities. Failing to stay on top of this could result in legal complications. When navigating the complexities of UK taxation, it is vital to understand the impact of recent tax reforms and any specific considerations relevant to the selling and reselling sector. Let us explore how taxes vary for sellers operating at different scales.

All information provided is specific to UK tax laws as of the 2024–2025 tax year. Tax rules vary significantly between countries, and what applies in the UK may not apply in other jurisdictions. If you reside or operate outside of the UK, you must do your own due diligence and consult local tax authorities or professionals to ensure compliance with your region's laws.

This is not tax advice. Make sure to do your own research even if you live in the UK

If you are just getting started with selling items, whether new or pre-owned, you might be making a little extra cash here and there, say £50 now and then. This can be a great way to boost your bank balance while learning and using a valuable skill. If you are earning less than £200 a month from selling or it is not your main source of income, you really do not have much to worry about from a tax perspective. In fact, the UK tax-free allowance, known as the Trading and Miscellaneous Income Allowance, is there to support people like you.

The Allowance

This allowance lets individuals earn up to £1,000 from trading or miscellaneous activities without needing to inform HM Revenue and Customs (HMRC) or pay tax on the profit. It's important to note that the allowance applies to profit, not income. While the term 'miscellaneous income allowance' might be confusing, as it includes 'income,' in tax terms it refers to the profit you make after subtracting expenses. As of the current tax year (2024-2025), the allowance is set at £1,000, but there are speculations that it could rise to £3,000 in the next tax year. Stay informed for updates after reading.

Income, also known as revenue, is the total money you receive from selling goods or services. It is the gross figure, with no deductions made yet. Profit is what's left once you subtract the money you spent to make those sales such as like buying stock, shipping and platform fees.

Tip: In everyday language the terms profit and income tend to get mixed up because they are used more loosely. In this context, when people say income, they may actually be referring to profit, even though in strict accounting terms they're different.

Remember, profit is what matters here, not your total sales income.

Let us clear it up by looking at an *example*:

Jay is seventeen and in his last year of college. Over a year Jay, sells items for a total of £1,400. That's his income (total revenue from sales).

But he was reselling these items for a profit and spent £800 on purchasing the items, shipping and platform fees. Those are his expenses.

Jay's profit = £1,400 (income) - £800 (expenses) = £600

For this allowance the £600 profit is what matters, not the £1,400 income.

If your profit exceeds £1,000 in a tax year, you will have to pay tax on the amount that exceeds £1,000. As Jay only made £600, he does not need to pay any tax.

If you are a beginner reselling on the side like Jay and you are only making a few hundred pounds, you don't need to worry too much about taxes unless your profit exceeds the £1,000 allowance.

Side Hustle

Jay's brother John made £5,000 in revenue in the same tax year, with a profit of £3,200 after expenses. John also works a part-time job three days a week, earning £15,000 a year from employment.

Let us explore how his tax situation looks and why it's different:

First, John's employment income of £15,000 is taxed separately through PAYE (Pay As You Earn) by his employer. This income uses up part of his Personal Allowance (£12,570 in 2024–2025), meaning he only pays tax on £2,430 of his job income (which is taxed at 20%). This is a total of £486.

Now, regarding his reselling profit of £3,200, the first £1,000 of this is covered by the Trading and Miscellaneous Income Allowance, leaving £2,200 taxable profit.

This £2,200 is added on top of the £15,000 from his job to calculate total income for the year (£17,200).

Since he's already used his £12,570 Personal Allowance, (which applies to overall income **different** from trading allowance), both the £2,430 from his job and the £2,200 from selling will be taxed at the basic 20% rate.

That means John will pay 20% tax on the £2,200 which is £440.

Summary:

John's job uses up his tax-free Personal Allowance, so after the £1,000 trading allowance, he still has taxable reselling profits. That's why, unlike Jay, who owes nothing, John pays £440 tax.

Disclaimer: This is **not** legal or financial advice. Tax situations vary and laws change. You should always consult a qualified accountant or tax professional before making any decisions about incorporation or tax planning.

 Tip: Whether you are engaged in reselling or simply clearing out items around the house, it is essential to maintain records. Even a basic list can be invaluable when calculating items sold, profit and revenue generated. Keeping organised records ensures accuracy and helps you stay on top of your finances.

The New 'Resellers' Tax

During the creation of this guide, the UK government announced changes to the reporting process for online resellers. This new tax has been dubbed the 'reseller tax,' as it appears the government is focusing on individuals who trade through online platforms. It has also attracted significant negative media attention. However, there's no actual new tax being introduced. What's changing is how information is reported to HMRC.

From 1st of January 2024, popular online marketplaces like the ones discussed in *Chapter Six* are now required to collect and report seller information to HMRC by January 2025. This agreement aims to ensure tax compliance and transparency in online transactions.

Rather than introducing a new tax, the government is simply tightening the rules for those who are actively selling online. Currently, meeting the criteria for this tax involves either selling 30 items online, though there is uncertainty about whether this is measured per platform or in total, or reaching £1,700 in sales. If you meet any of those two requirements, your information will be shared with HMRC.

This doesn't automatically mean you will receive a tax bill, but if you are earning a significant income from selling, you may be required to pay tax on your profits, as you likely would have been already. The way tax is treated

and paid is explained in the two previous examples in the last section. The goal for the government is to differentiate between occasional personal sales and more consistent, profit-driven activities using the data these platforms now have to provide for them.

Challenges

The specifics of how these changes will unfold are still unclear, and it's difficult to offer precise guidance on how they will impact everyone. It's important to stay informed as the government moves forward with enforcing these changes, ensuring you remain compliant with any potential tax liabilities.

The practical challenges in implementing and enforcing this tax are significant. One of the main issues is distinguishing between professional traders and individuals selling personal items. For example, someone selling £3,000 worth of belongings while moving house may not make a profit but could still fall under the threshold for the tax. How the government will distinguish between these scenarios is still uncertain.

Tip: Selling old items you own or things from around the house is a great way to start. It helps generate positive reviews and much-needed capital.

Another challenge arises with sales conducted in cash, such as those made through meetups or in-person exchanges. These transactions can be difficult to track and verify for profits, further complicating enforcement.

The government is simply tightening enforcement on individuals who are selling online and not reporting their profits or paying tax. If you were not earning enough to pay tax before, the same rules still apply. Similarly, if you were already paying tax on your profits from online sales, the amount or rate you pay remains unchanged.

What is changing is that digital platforms are now required to report seller information to HMRC. However, it is still unclear how the government will enforce this in certain scenarios.

How will they track in-person or cash sales? How will they address situations where sellers make losses, and how could they even know? These are just some of the many questions that need clarification as the system is rolled out as its unclear how the tax will be applied in these scenarios.

Overall, while this is not technically a new tax, it adds another layer of complexity. As the system is rolled out, the government needs to address these practical enforcement challenges. In the meantime, it is important to stay informed and take advantage of official resources, such as government websites and helplines, to understand your responsibilities. If you are generating significant profits through reselling, you may now fall within tax thresholds, and staying compliant will help avoid any future penalties. Tax rules continue to evolve, so keeping up to date and assessing your situation regularly is essential.

Conclusion

Once you find your hustle has solid foundations and steady growth, the focus shifts from simply making it work to deciding how far you want to take it. Whether you grow through the methods above or others you discover, what began as a side project can quickly become a serious operation. Expansion means stepping back, looking at the bigger picture and making decisions that could raise your potential. Whether that means reinvesting, building systems, or outsourcing, these choices can shape your next phase.

As your growth continues, the original structure of a sole trader flipping items on the side may no longer be enough. You may need to consider how your business is set up, not just how it runs. The next chapter will guide you through formalising your operation. It covers limited companies, partnerships, and other structures, showing how the right setup can support your ambitions and help you go further.

Keep in mind, this next chapter is short, quite advanced, and only relevant for a small section of readers who are seriously scaling up. Newcomers can safely skip it for now.

Chapter Summary

❖ We examine cook groups, their benefits, costs, where to find them, and how to avoid red flags when joining.

❖ Bulk buying lets you purchase large quantities at lower prices to boost profits and maintain steady stock. Reece's example shows how patience and a solid plan can make this strategy work.

❖ Getting support from family or friends can help you start or grow your business. Be clear about your plan and offer a fair return. The example of Jack and Jane shows how a small loan and trust can lead to success for both sides. This approach helps build trust and access funds to expand.

❖ We look at how the new 'reseller tax' isn't actually a new tax, but just the government changing legislation to require marketplaces to share selling information with HMRC.

❖ The £1,000 trading and miscellaneous income allowance allows individuals to earn up to this amount from side activities without paying tax, and we compare how it applies to people with different income levels.

Chapter Ten

Entities

As mentioned previously, this chapter covers more advanced topics that are mainly relevant to those looking to scale their operations in a serious way. Even if you are just starting out, the concepts in this chapter offer useful knowledge that can help later if you decide to grow or pursue other ventures. It is also good to understand how the business world works and have a general idea of what is going on around you.

This chapter is called *Entities* because it goes beyond the basics to explore different business structures and how they affect operations. First, we will look at incorporation, what it involves and why it may be beneficial for those processing large volumes or generating substantial revenue.

Next, we will look at partnerships, how they work, and why some people choose them instead of forming a limited company. They come with their own unique benefits that can suit different goals or situations. Again, while this information is more relevant to serious sellers, it still gives beginners useful insight into why businesses are structured in certain ways. Whether it is limited companies and **PLC**s in the UK or LLCs in the US, understanding these choices helps you make better decisions about your own business.

Incorporation

What is Incorporation?

Incorporation is the process of registering your business as a separate legal entity. This separates you legally and financially from the business, allowing it to own property, enter contracts, incur liabilities and pay taxes in its own name.

For most small businesses, incorporation usually means moving from sole trader status to a limited (Ltd) company. This step provides a multitude of benefits which we will go through. You can pay yourself through a combination of ways to potentially reduce your tax burden compared to operating as a sole trader.

Incorporation is often most suitable for those generating consistent profits or planning to grow their business. It does come with added paperwork, formal responsibilities, and costs, so for casual earners it may not always be worth it. If you fit the criteria, consulting a tax advisor can help determine whether incorporation is the right move.

Who Should Consider Incorporation?

Incorporation isn't necessary for everyone, especially when starting out, but there are certain types of sellers and business situations where it becomes particularly advantageous. These include:

Consistent High-Volume Sellers: If you are regularly processing hundreds of orders or generating significant monthly revenue, operating as a limited company can make more sense than remaining a sole trader. This structure can help you manage and optimise your tax liabilities more effectively, taking advantage of corporate tax rates and potential deductions that may not be available to sole traders.

Expansion Plans: For sellers planning to scale their operations, incorporation can provide a solid foundation for growth. A corporate structure facilitates easier access to capital through various means, such as selling shares or applying for loans.

Additionally, it enhances your business's professional image, boosting credibility and making it more attractive to larger customers or potential partners.

Credible Image: Some sellers may want the added credibility and professionalism that comes with being a registered company, especially when dealing with suppliers, clients, or partners who prefer to work with established businesses.

Why Incorporate?

Incorporating your business offers a range of advantages beyond just formality. While it may not be essential for everyone, those operating at scale or aiming for long-term growth can benefit significantly:

Limited Liability: Often the main reason people incorporate, it protects your personal assets if the business faces financial or legal trouble. This makes it a key benefit for anyone looking to grow while keeping their personal wealth secure.

Professional Image: Operating as a limited company often lends more credibility to your business. It signals to clients, suppliers, and partners that your business is established and serious. This can be especially helpful when dealing with larger companies or securing contracts where an incorporated status is preferred or even required.

Access to Capital: Incorporated businesses often have more options for raising funds. Whether through issuing shares, attracting investors, or accessing different types of loans, incorporation opens the door to more financing opportunities that can fuel business growth.

Continuity and Succession: Unlike sole trader businesses, a company is a separate legal entity, which means it can continue to operate regardless of changes in ownership or management. This is useful for succession planning, selling the business, or even bringing in new shareholders over time.

Tax Efficiency: Companies are taxed differently from individuals. Incorporation allows access to corporate tax rates, which may be lower than personal income tax rates, depending on your profit levels. You can claim a wider range of business expenses and potentially retain profits in the company to reinvest, rather than withdrawing everything as personal income.

Example: Say you are a sole trader earning £50,000 a year. As a sole trader, all your profits are treated as personal income, so you pay income tax and National Insurance on the full amount.

In the 2023-2024 tax year, anything you earn over £50,270 is taxed at 40%, and even the income below that is taxed in stages: 20% for basic rate and 12%+ for National Insurance. That can add up quickly.

Now you decide to incorporate. As the owner of a limited company, you can choose how much to pay yourself as a salary and how much to take as dividends. Many directors pay themselves a small salary, usually just under the personal allowance threshold of £12,570 so it is tax-free and keeps National Insurance low.

The rest of the profit, in this case around £37,430, stays in the company. The company pays corporation tax on that profit at 19%, which would be £7,111, leaving around £30,319. You could then take this remaining money out as dividends, which are taxed at lower rates than salary income. The remaining profit can be paid out as dividends, taxed at lower rates than salary.

You also get to claim a wider range of business expenses like office equipment, travel, and software, reducing taxable profit further.

This setup gives you much more control. Instead of being taxed on the full £50,000 as a sole trader, you are using a mix of salary and dividends to reduce how much tax you pay overall.

Comparison

Sole trader:

You pay income tax and National Insurance on the full £50,000. For the 2023/24 tax year, this means:

- Income tax of £7,486 and national Insurance contributions of about £3,774.

Total tax: £11,260

Incorporated:

You pay yourself a salary of £12,570 tax-free (personal allowance).

- The remaining £37,430 is company profit and taxed at 19% corporation tax = £7,111.

If you take the rest as dividends instead of reinvesting, for this example, the dividend tax on the £30,319 after corporation tax, at 8.75% basic rate, is about £2,650.

But if you keep all the profits in the business and do not withdraw dividends, you only pay the £7,111 corporation tax now and retain £30,319 in the company to reinvest or withdraw later.

Total tax if taking dividends: £9,752

Total tax if keeping profits in the company: £7,111

Money you keep:

- Sole trader: £38,740.
- Incorporated taking dividends: £40,498.
- Incorporated keeping profits in the company: £42,319.

Incorporation could save you around £1,750 to £3,500 in taxes on £50,000 profit, depending on how much you withdraw, plus it allows you to reinvest profits and claim more business expenses.

Disclaimer: *This example assumes all profits are taken as salary and dividends in a straightforward way. Actual tax depends on your specific situation and may vary. Always consult a tax professional for advice.*

Incorporation is strategic move that provides stability, growth potential, and long-term benefits as your business evolves. It offers significant advantages, especially if you are making substantial profits, by creating a structured path for growth, improving tax management and protecting your personal assets, making it a valuable step for those looking to take their business to the next level.

Services

Another major advantage of being incorporated is access to services not available to sole traders. Incorporation gives you entry to business-only services such as:

- **Business Banking Accounts**: Many traditional banks offer business banking services that include features like business loans, credit lines and specialised financial products not available to personal account holders.
- **Business Credit Cards**: Business credit cards offer higher credit limits, expense management tools and rewards tailored to business spending. They provide features like employee card management and business-specific benefits.
- **Wholesale Pricing and Bulk Discounts**: Businesses often have access to wholesale pricing and bulk discounts from suppliers and manufacturers which are not available to individual consumers.

Royal Mail Business Account

As an example, a Royal Mail business account, available exclusively to those sending at least 20 parcels a week or incorporated businesses, is designed to enhance logistics efficiency and cost management. Here's how a Royal Mail business account can help:

- **Discounted Rates**: Business accounts often come with reduced shipping rates, which can significantly cut down your overall costs, especially when dealing with high volumes.
- **Streamlined Shipping Process**: Tools provided by Royal Mail for business account holders can simplify the shipping process. This includes bulk shipping options, automated label printing and scheduled pickups, saving you valuable time.
- **Reliable Delivery**: Ensuring timely deliveries is crucial for maintaining a strong reputation. Royal Mail's robust network helps ensure that your products reach customers promptly and reliably.
- **Tracking and Reporting**: Enhanced tracking features and detailed reporting tools allow you to monitor shipments and

manage customer expectations effectively. This transparency is key to providing excellent customer service and handling any delivery issues that arise.

In summary, managing your logistics through services only available to incorporated business can streamline your operations, reduce costs and enhance customer satisfaction.

Partnerships

Now that we have covered incorporation and what it involves, let us turn to another common business structure: partnerships. Unlike limited companies, partnerships involve two or more people working together to run a business without creating a separate legal entity.

This structure is often chosen when people want to combine their skills, resources, and responsibilities without the formalities of incorporation. Partnerships and limited companies are the two main options for most small to medium ventures. Public limited companies (PLCs), which are listed on the stock exchange and represent some of the biggest companies in the world, are of a much larger scale and are not the focus of this guide.

What is a Partnership?

A partnership is a legal arrangement where two or more people run a business together. Unlike a company, a partnership is not a separate legal entity. Instead, the partners share responsibility for the business, including profits, losses and liabilities. Partnerships are often chosen when people want to combine skills, resources or capital to run a business without setting up a full company.

Why Do Partnerships Exist?

Partnerships allow people to work together to share the workload, risks and rewards of a business. They are common where different skills or expertise complement each other.

In a partnership, profit splits are usually arranged through a formal agreement between the partners. This agreement, called a partnership agreement, outlines how profits (and losses) will be divided. It does not have to be a 50–50 split.

The partners can agree on any ratio that reflects their contributions, responsibilities, or what they feel is fair.

Example: Sarah brings in most of the clients and handles the bulk of the creative work, while Tom focuses more on the business admin side. They might agree that Sarah should receive 60% of the profits and Tom 40%. This would be written clearly in their agreement to avoid confusion later.

So, if their business earns £8,000 in profit one month, that agreement would mean Sarah gets £4,800 and Tom gets £3,200. This flexibility is one of the key benefits of a partnership structure, as it allows people to tailor how rewards are shared based on the reality of who is doing what.

Key Benefits of Partnerships

- Shared responsibility and decision making.
- Easier and cheaper to set up than companies.
- Combined skills and capital can help grow the business.
- Flexible profit-sharing arrangements
- Avoids some formal corporate requirements.

Partnerships benefit people who want to pool their resources and share business responsibilities without the formalities of incorporating. They suit professionals, small business owners and anyone who values working closely with trusted partners. Because partnerships do not offer limited liability, they are better suited for low-risk businesses or where partners know each other well.

While most partnerships are formed for professional or financial reasons, the core motivation is often simple. People come together to do more than they could alone. Whether it is pooling money, sharing knowledge, dividing tasks or just having someone to work with, partnerships help reduce pressure and increase potential.

Most partnerships follow traditional setups such as through law or accountancy firms.

If two aspiring sellers each have limited funds but combine their capital, they can invest in more profitable purchases that would have otherwise been out of reach and share the risk and responsibility Similarly, teaming up with a friend to manage sourcing, listing, and shipping can help divide responsibilities, increase productivity, and grow at a faster rate.

Considerations

If you are earning money online, running a small business or building any kind of income stream outside of traditional employment, understanding how tax works is essential.

Your decision on how to proceed should be based on your individual circumstances and where you are in your journey. Laws and regulations can change, so it's important to conduct your own research and consult with professionals if needed.

The key message from this chapters is: tax matters, and your business structure affects how you manage it. For low-income or part-time ventures, staying as a sole trader might be fine. Just be clear about your responsibilities.

For high earning or long-term plans, incorporation or a partnership could offer better protection and flexibility. What matters most is that you stay transparent, keep good records and build on the right foundation. There is no single best option, only the one that suits where you are and where you want to go.

Chapter Summary

❖ Incorporation: what it is, who should consider it, and the main benefits it offers for those scaling up.

❖ We break down the tax efficiency of being incorporated and outline the different services and protections available to LTDs.

❖ What partnerships are, who they suit, how they work, and why some people choose them instead of forming a limited company.

❖ We highlight key tax points and structural factors to consider, to help you make better long-term decisions.

Chapter Eleven

Restoration

Restoration is where reselling meets craftsmanship. It is not just about finding cheap items and flipping them but about improving what you find to increase its value before selling. Whether it is cleaning, repairing or repackaging, restoration adds another layer to traditional reselling, and with it, the potential for greater profits. These extra steps can transform items that others overlook into highly desirable products. This chapter explores how adding value through restoration can set you apart in competitive markets, help you build niche expertise and, ultimately, unlock bigger returns. Let us start by looking at how this model works across different types of products.

For example, consider someone who repairs watches or fixes snapped golf clubs. People are willing to pay for these services. But there's another angle: what if you bought a broken watch at a low price, used your skills to restore it, and sold it at a much higher price? By applying your expertise, you are not only enhancing the item but significantly increasing your profit margin. This can be a powerful business model.

By focusing on one area over time, you can build a reputation, whether for restoring, flipping or both. With consistency and quality, you become the person others trust in that niche.

A good example of this model is Golf-bidder, which started as a small shop dealing in used golf clubs. Over time, by specialising in refurbishing and reselling golf equipment, it grew into a well-known platform and is now the go-to place for buying and selling golf clubs.

Other example niches where the same logic can be applied include:

- Bicycles.
- Furniture.
- Smartphones and tablets.
- Laptops and PCs.
- Cameras and lenses.
- Sneakers and shoes.
- Car parts.
- Musical instruments (e.g., guitars, keyboards).
- Designer accessories.
- Jewellery.
- Video game consoles.
- Collectible toys.
- Home appliances (e.g., coffee machines, blenders).
- Lawn equipment (e.g., mowers, trimmers).
- Vintage electronics (e.g., radios, record players).
- Paintings or artwork (framing, touch-ups).
- Clothing (cleaning, repairs, alterations).

These examples show how restoration can be applied across different product categories. Whether it is sneakers, sports gear, electronics or furniture, the strategy of buying, improving and reselling for profit remains consistent.

By developing skills in one area, you create a foundation that can expand into others, opening up new markets and increasing your potential returns.

Next, we will dive deep into one effective method: sneaker restoration, with a focus on addressing the common issue of outsole yellowing. By restoring and improving the condition of sneakers, especially those with discoloured outsoles, you can greatly enhance their resale value and dramatically increase your profit margins.

The Sole Icing Guide

The passage of time can have a noticeable effect on sneakers, particularly on their outsoles. Sneakers with white or translucent outsoles are especially prone to developing an undesirable yellowish look due to prolonged exposure to air and light, a natural oxidation process.

This yellowing can significantly diminish the overall aesthetic appeal. What may seem like a drawback can be turned into a profitable opportunity through a process known as '**icing**.' This tried-and-true method restores yellowed outsoles to their original, vibrant condition, effectively reversing the discolouration and enhancing the value of the sneakers.

By offering sole icing services or flipping sneakers with yellowed soles after icing them, resellers can tap into this niche market, breathing new life into worn-out sneakers and bringing them closer to their original pristine state. This transformation is particularly beneficial for iconic models like the Jordan 11, where outsole yellowing can significantly impact their overall appearance.

 Tip: Building relationships within the sneaker community or your specific niche is crucial. By cultivating connections with fellow people in your niche, you can provide specialised services to them.

To illustrate how this plays out, imagine a scenario where George purchases a pair of used Jordan 11s. These have a market value of £300 but require careful evaluation of their condition. Assuming the Jordans are in good condition with only minor wear and a yellowed sole, their estimated value could be around £120, significantly lower than the price of a new pair. By negotiating with the seller, George manages to acquire them for £100. This presents an opportunity for a quick flip, even if he chooses not to address the yellowed soles.

Employing the icing process to enhance the appearance of the sole can substantially increase the sneakers' value. After revitalisation, the pair may now fetch around £170 due to its improved condition, resulting in a net profit of £70. This profit easily covers any variable costs, as explored later in this chapter. It's essential to note that this process can be repeated multiple times and applied to several sneakers simultaneously, depending on the capacity of the ice box used.

Nonetheless, understand that the examples provided represent estimations of best-case scenarios, as real-world outcomes can vary.

Essential Tools

In the next section, we will discuss the importance of the **ice box** in the icing process. This tool is essential for sole restoration.

What exactly is an 'ice box?'

An ice box is designed to assist in the restoration of sneaker soles by using controlled temperature and humidity to reverse yellowing. We will explore the step-by-step process of building an ice box, the materials you will need, and the science behind its effectiveness.

Additionally, the chapter provides a cost analysis, helping you understand the expenses involved so you can make an informed decision. Additionally, we will touch on the potential return on investment (ROI) and how to troubleshoot common challenges that may arise during the sole icing process. With this knowledge, you can maximise the financial returns from your investment while ensuring your sneakers receive the best possible care.

Investing in an ice box is a crucial step for anyone serious about sneaker restoration, particularly in the process of sole icing. While it requires an upfront financial commitment, the long-term benefits can far outweigh the initial costs.

Necessary Materials

Item	Purpose	Cost
Cardboard box	Enclosure to contain the process and fit multiple pairs.	£20
UV Light (800W)	Simulates sunlight for oxidation process.	£60
Sole sauce	Solution responsible for deoxidation.	£30
Fan	Cools sneakers to prevent damage during process.	£60
Misc. supplies	Tinfoil, cling film, paintbrush, tape. Necessary for wrapping, protecting soles and assembling the box.	£20
Total		**£190**

💡 **Tip:** Using multiple UV lights can speed up the deoxidation process by providing more consistent coverage. However, this increases the overall cost and may require additional fans to manage heat, so balance efficiency with your budget and setup space.

Setting up an ice box typically requires a budget of around £200, but with resourcefulness and cost-saving measures, it can be achieved for approximately £120, especially if you already possess some of the necessary items or can find them at a lower cost. All figures mentioned above have been rounded up for the sake of prudence. In certain cases, the total expenditure for specific ice boxes may reach up to £300. This higher cost primarily stems from the construction of larger ice boxes, which offer the advantage of simultaneously icing multiple pairs of sneakers. If your goal is to profit from flipping a large volume of sneakers using this method, building a bigger ice box is crucial.

It's worth noting that while individual costs may vary slightly, each component plays a significant role in constructing an effective ice box.

 Tip: When searching for components like lighting and fans for your ice box, consider exploring the second-hand market through different platforms and apply the precautions outlined in *Chapter Four* when engaging in transactions within the second-hand market.

Cost Considerations

The expenses associated with ice box creation extend beyond the initial purchase of components and need to be kept in mind.

Electricity Costs

Operating an ice box can be quite costly. The deoxidation process sessions can vary in duration, ranging from six hours to potentially as long as twenty hours, depending on the extent of yellowing and the desired results. During these sessions, both the UV lights and the fans you choose to incorporate will consume electricity. For instance, if you are running an 800W UV light for twelve hours, it might use around 9.6 kWh (kilowatt-hours). The average cost of electricity in the UK is approximately £0.27 per kWh as of 2025. Therefore, running the UV light for twelve hours could cost you around £2.59.

It is important to multiply this by the number of lights and fans you are using and the duration of each session to gauge your electricity expenses accurately and bear them in mind when calculating profit margins. Keep in mind that the actual cost may vary depending on factors such as equipment efficiency and regional electricity rates, so always verify specific details for the equipment you are using.

Prebuilt Purchase Considerations

While building your box offers a cost-effective approach, it's worth noting that you can find ready-made ice boxes available for purchase online. These ready-made options are usually more expensive than assembling your own, but they come with the convenience of not having to construct the box yourself. They are typically manufactured to a high standard, ensuring they meet the required specifications for effective sole icing. This option is ideal for those who may be unwilling, or lack the necessary time, to put effort into building their ice box from scratch. You do pay for the convenience as these are typically higher in price.

Maintenance and Replacement Costs

Over time, UV lights and fans may require maintenance or replacement due to extended use. These costs should be factored into the overall expenditure for operating the ice box in the context of sole icing. Proper maintenance ensures the continued effectiveness of your ice box. These are your running costs and will happen overtime.

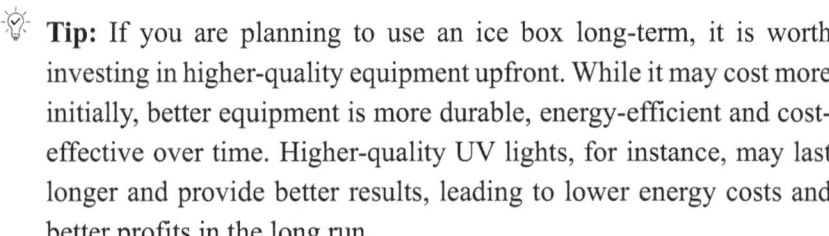 **Tip:** If you are planning to use an ice box long-term, it is worth investing in higher-quality equipment upfront. While it may cost more initially, better equipment is more durable, energy-efficient and cost-effective over time. Higher-quality UV lights, for instance, may last longer and provide better results, leading to lower energy costs and better profits in the long run.

By considering these cost factors, you can make informed decisions throughout the process, ensuring that you optimise your investment while understanding the potential costs involved. Although these costs may seem small individually, they can accumulate quickly and need to be carefully considered when planning your budget and calculating potential profits.

Building Your Ice Box

Step 1: Assemble the Box

The first step is to put the cardboard box together. Make sure the box is in good condition and sturdy, as it will house your sneakers during the deoxidation process.

Step 2: Line the Interior with Tin Foil

To maximise the reflection of UV light within the box, line the interior with tin foil. This step helps contain the light, preventing it from escaping.

Be meticulous in ensuring that the entire inside surface is covered in tin foil.

Step 3: Cut Off Ends

If your box has flaps, cut them off. This allows the UV light to sit on the top of the box, minimising the amount of light escaping and ensuring even exposure for the sneakers' soles.

Step 4: Create a Door

Using a utility knife, cut out a door on the side of the box. This door allows you to easily place your sneakers inside and take them out after the icing process is complete. Make sure it's large enough to comfortably fit your sneakers.

Step 5: Add an Air Hole for the Fan

To facilitate air circulation and prevent the sneakers from overheating, create a small air hole in your box. You can use a thermometer to monitor the temperature inside. It is crucial to keep it below 28 degrees Celsius (83 degrees Fahrenheit) to prevent damage to your sneakers.

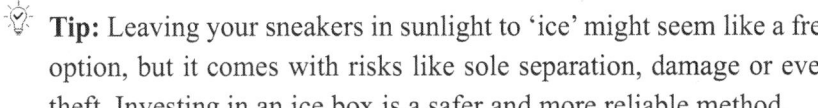 **Tip:** Leaving your sneakers in sunlight to 'ice' might seem like a free option, but it comes with risks like sole separation, damage or even theft. Investing in an ice box is a safer and more reliable method.

Step 6: Position the UV Light

Place the UV light at the top of the box. Ensure its securely fastened and any holes or gaps around the light are taped up to prevent light from escaping.

Step 7: Prepare Your Sneakers

Before placing your sneakers in the box, make sure they are clean. Remove any dirt or debris from the soles to ensure optimal results during the process.

Step 8: Apply Sole Sauce

Using a thin paintbrush, generously apply the **sole sauce** to the yellowed areas of your sneakers' soles. This solution will initiate the deoxidation process, gradually restoring the original colour of the soles.

Step 9: Wrap in Cling Film

After applying the sole sauce, wrap your sneakers in cling film. This step preserves moisture and allowing the deoxidation process to work effectively.

Step 10: Allow for Deoxidation

Place the wrapped sneakers inside your ice box and leave them undisturbed for a duration ranging from six to twenty-four hours. The specific time needed depends on the severity of the yellowing, so be patient and monitor the progress.

Step 11: Rinse and Clean

Once you are satisfied with the results, carefully remove the plastic wrap from your sneakers' soles and rinse them thoroughly with water. This removes any residual hydrogen peroxide, and you can now allow your sneakers to air dry.

Step 12: Enjoy Your Revived Soles

With the completion of the sole icing process, your sneakers' soles should have regained their original colour, or at least a significant portion of it. Enjoy the refreshed look of your kicks as they return to their former glory.

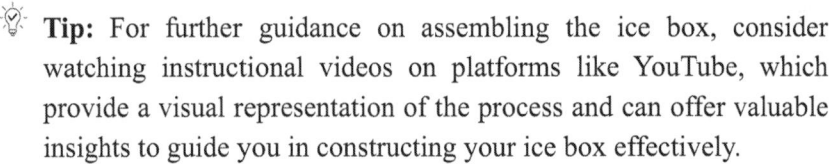 **Tip:** For further guidance on assembling the ice box, consider watching instructional videos on platforms like YouTube, which provide a visual representation of the process and can offer valuable insights to guide you in constructing your ice box effectively.

Important Considerations

- **Safety First:** Always handle the sole sauce with care. Wear protective gear such as gloves and safety goggles and use knives cautiously. If you are underage, make sure to ask an adult for assistance. Additionally, always work in a well-ventilated area to avoid exposure to harmful fumes.
- **Trial and Error:** If the yellowing is extensive, you may need to repeat the process several times to achieve your desired results.
- **UV Light Source:** The strength of the UV light source matters. Natural sunlight can work, but a UV lamp designed for this purpose may yield faster results.

Remember that sole deoxidation is a DIY process, and the outcome depends on multiple factors. Be patient and take precautions to avoid any mishaps during the restoration process.

Mistakes to Learn From

Even though sole icing can be highly effective, it is a process that requires precision, patience, and a proper setup. When something goes wrong, whether due to poor preparation, skipping steps, or overlooking safety measures, the consequences can wipe out your effort and profit in one go.

Imagine restoring a pair of Jordan 11s with yellowed soles. You clean them, apply the sole sauce, wrap them up and place them in your ice box. But the temperature inside the box rises too high because there is no airflow or thermometer. Hours later, the midsoles have warped, or the soles have begun to separate from the uppers. At that point, not only have you failed to restore the sneaker, but you may have damaged it beyond resale value. What could have been a profitable project turns into a loss, and worse, a wasted opportunity.

That is why learning to troubleshoot is just as important as learning the method. The following table covers common restoration mistakes and how to avoid them, helping you protect both your time and your investment.

161

Problem	Likely Cause	Solution
Lack of colour change	Weak UV light, poor reflection, or expired sole sauce.	Upgrade UV lamp (800W+), re-layer foil, or replace sauce.
Overheating / sole separation	Box too hot, no ventilation.	Add a fan, open air holes, and monitor with a thermometer.
Streaky or uneven results	Dirty soles, uneven application, no cling film.	Thoroughly clean before applying, use quality brush, and wrap tightly.
Hardened or dried sauce	Left too long or poor wrapping .	Shorten exposure or improve cling film seal.
Light escaping from box	Gaps in box lid or corners.	Seal all edges with tape or reconfigure box design.

While sole icing is one of the most accessible and effective ways to restore sneakers, it is just the beginning. Once you gain confidence using this method, you may find yourself exploring other ways to add value through restoration. From simple cleaning to more advanced repairs, each technique opens new opportunities to revive worn sneakers and maximise profits. Below are some of the most common and impactful sneaker restoration methods beyond sole icing.

Other Restoration Techniques

Cleaning

A fundamental restoration technique, 'cleaning' involves restoring sneakers to their former glory through meticulous cleaning. This process might include removing dirt, grime and stains from uppers, midsoles and outsoles. Various cleaning agents, brushes and techniques are employed.

Sole Swaps and Re-gluing

Sole swaps replace damaged or worn-out soles with new or compatible ones, giving a fresh foundation to a pair that might otherwise be unsellable. Re-gluing fixes soles separating from the upper, requiring the right adhesive and careful application. Both techniques can revive sneakers and are valuable skills for any restorer

Re-painting

Repainting is another aspect of sneaker restoration, involving the application of fresh paint to areas where the original colour has faded or chipped. This meticulous process requires careful colour matching and precise application techniques to achieve a seamless finish, effectively revitalising the overall appearance of the sneakers.

Customisation

Designers have built successful businesses by customising sneakers. While this requires a high level of skill and creativity, it can be a lucrative niche once you've honed your craft. With enough expertise, you can transform ordinary sneakers into unique, in-demand pieces, which can significantly increase their value.

Each of these advanced restoration techniques offers resellers another chance to revive worn-out sneakers and turn them into valuable assets. However, unlike the relatively straightforward process of using an ice box for sole icing, techniques like sole swaps and re-gluing require a high level of skill, meticulous practice and a deep understanding of sneaker construction. These methods are not for the faint of heart, they are tedious, risky, and can be costly if not executed properly. For those without the necessary talent or experience, attempting these techniques can lead to irreparable damage. That said, for those who master them, these skills can open up new avenues in sneaker restoration, allowing you to breathe life into sneakers that others might overlook, whether as a passionate hobbyist or a profit-driven reseller.

While this guide is focused on sneaker restoration, the principles behind it can be applied to a wide range of items as mentioned earlier, making it a versatile strategy for anyone looking to profit from flipping or restoring goods. The core method remains consistent: buy low, invest time and effort into improving the product, and sell high for a profit.

Chapter Summary

❖ You can profit from restoration by offering a service or using your skills to add value and resell items for a profit.

❖ A list of different ways to profit from restoration and using examples like Golf-bidder, which grew by refurbishing and selling second-hand golf clubs.

❖ A comprehensive guide to sole icing, covering all the details and techniques involved.

❖ Other popular restoration techniques including cleaning, regluing, repainting and customisation.

Chapter Twelve

Bot Technology

Bot technology has become a powerful tool in various industries, from ticket sales to high-demand drops, where securing limited items is crucial. However, it's within the sneaker community that botting has truly cemented its place as an advanced, and sometimes controversial, practice.

This chapter will cover what botting is, why it exists and how it works. As with earlier chapters, we will use the sneaker industry as an example, since it is heavily affected by botting. You will gain an understanding of how botting operates, the financial risks involved and the common mistakes people make. Rather than focusing on a specific bot, this chapter offers a general overview of botting. The goal is not to provide a detailed manual for any particular bot, as the niche is wide-ranging and constantly changing.

WARNING - This chapter is for those deeply entrenched in their specific niche such as sneaker culture. Botting is an advanced practice requiring extensive knowledge, significant capital and patience. Botting is recommended only for those with the expertise and resources to navigate its complexities, as diving in unprepared can lead to significant challenges. Assess your readiness carefully before venturing into this advanced area.

What it is

'Botting' represents a phenomenon in the sneaker and fashion industries, emerging as an approach to acquire limited editions during releases, drops, and raffles. At its core, botting involves the use of specialised software, commonly known as bots, designed to automate the purchasing process on various online platforms. These tools provide users with a distinct advantage by streamlining the checkout process, thereby increasing their chances of securing highly sought-after apparel and a higher quantity at that.

Why do it?

Simply, profit. The primary motivation behind botting is the potential for substantial financial gains. Limited edition drops often generate extraordinary demand, creating a lucrative resale market. Using bots allows individuals to secure multiple items during releases. This creates an opportunity to capitalise on demand by selling more products at inflated prices.

Botting also increases the likelihood of successfully securing multiple items during releases and raffles. Traditional manual methods may not yield the same level of success due to high competition and limited availability. Bots streamline the purchasing process, enabling users to win multiple pairs, a deciding factor and advantage, only adding to profit.

Other advantages include:

Sell In Bulk: Getting multiple items through botting lets individuals sell in bulk, boosting profits and establishing trust as reliable suppliers. This creates a sustainable business model. For example, winning five sneakers means having ready buyers who are willing to purchase each pair at a markup. This quick turnover allows for instant sales and builds lasting relationships with buyers, making bulk selling a straightforward and effective approach.

Build a Larger Customer Base: Consistently successful botting not only secures apparel but also cultivates a reputation for reliability within your niche's community. By repeatedly acquiring and offering sought-after releases, sellers can expand their customer base. This reliability fosters trust and ensures a steady stream of customers for future releases.

Understanding Bot Terms and Practices

To comprehend the details of botting, let us familiarise ourselves with some terms and practices, ranging from the straightforward to the more complex:

- **The Bot:** The pivotal software that automates most tasks, enabling users to enter drops and raffles with multiple accounts from a single device, simulating activity from various sources.
- **Subscription:** Some bots operate on a subscription basis, requiring monthly, half-yearly, or annual payments. The subscription model varies among bots, with some opting for non-subscription services.
- **Proxies:** Specialised servers that enhance the anonymity and efficiency of sneaker bots during online releases. **Proxies** act as intermediaries between the bot and the sneaker store's server, concealing real IP addresses. They play a crucial role in avoiding restrictions, preventing IP bans, and executing multiple requests discreetly, thereby enhancing bot performance.
- **Different Accounts/Emails:** A common strategy involving the use of multiple accounts and unique emails to bypass purchase restrictions set by retailers. This enables bot users to increase their chances of copping.
- **Different Cards:** Utilising diverse credit cards for each transaction is a preventive measure against cancellations and increases the likelihood of successful purchases. This helps avoid suspicion from retailers, as multiple purchases with the same card may be flagged.
- **Servers (Circumstantial):** Employing different servers becomes beneficial, especially during high-traffic releases. This approach helps distribute bot activity, mitigating the risk of IP bans and enhancing overall performance. The decision to use multiple servers is circumstantial, depending on the scale and nature of botting activities.
- **Different Addresses:** Major help for avoiding detection, using various shipping addresses (not the same as IP) helps distribute

purchases more evenly and reduces the risk of being flagged for suspicious activity. This strategy aligns with retailers' restrictions on the number of purchases per address.

Having covered account setup and proxies, let's now examine a detection-evasion strategy commonly known as 'jigging'.

Jigging

'**jigging,**' often stylised as 'j1gging', is a manoeuvre in the botting world where individuals modify certain details to make them appear unique, preventing detection by retailer sites that aim to detect automated bot activity.

This usually means altering addresses, names, and other details with small changes or random characters. Often written as j1gging to avoid detection, it is not recommended due to the risks, but we will still cover it because of how common it is.

Why J1gging?

Online retailer sites employ stringent measures to combat bots, scrutinising every purchase for potential automated activity. If they detect multiple orders with identical details, especially addresses, it raises red flags, leading to immediate cancellation of the botter's purchases. Jigging aims to circumvent this detection by making seemingly identical addresses appear different, enabling bot users to make multiple purchases without triggering automated anti-bot responses.

Details Subject to J1gging

J1gging isn't restricted to addresses alone. Bot users may employ this strategy for various details, including names, emails, shipping addresses, phone numbers, and even credit card numbers.

Cautionary Note: Jigging can cause multiple issues for those engaging in it.

These can include:

- **Parcels Misdelivered**: Altering information can lead to mis-deliveries, causing complications and potential loss of purchased items.
- **Platform Bans:** Multiple purchases with jigged details can result in bans on various platforms and retailers. These can occur with the perpetrator being unaware of the ban.
- **Parcel Claiming Challenges:** J1gging may make it challenging to claim parcels, especially if details are altered significantly.

Examples

- Real Address: 31 Ashwood Road
- Jigged Address: AJSH 31 @swood Road, 031 Ashwood Rd.

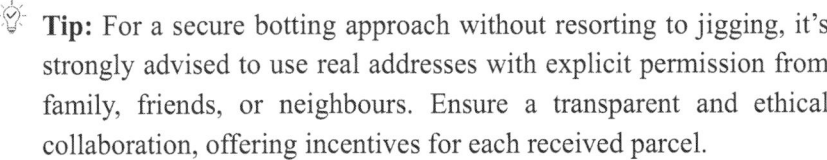 **Tip:** For a secure botting approach without resorting to jigging, it's strongly advised to use real addresses with explicit permission from family, friends, or neighbours. Ensure a transparent and ethical collaboration, offering incentives for each received parcel.

While this section intends to give a full overview, j1gging is not something recommended due to its risks. It is generally discouraged within the community because of the problems it can cause for individuals and the wider industry. Although some still use it, success depends on very careful execution. It is being included here so you are fully informed and aware of the risks involved. With that covered, we can now move on to explore the different paths people take within botting.

Different Paths

In botting there is two primary avenues: drop and raffle botting. Raffle botting, although more common, is more UK-specific. Let us explore both and the strategies and considerations that come with.

Tip: Many bots are not readily available on the market and often have waiting lists. It's advisable to stay informed about release schedules and join waiting lists promptly to increase your chances of obtaining a bot when it becomes available.

Drop Botting

Drop botting comes into play when products are released on a set schedule or through shock drops, catching users off guard. The primary objective is swift and multiple checkouts before they sell out. While less common in the UK, drop botting remains a quality strategy for securing releases.

Raffle Botting

Raffle botting takes centre stage, especially in the UK. This is the method that involves simultaneously entering multiple accounts into a raffle, elevating the chances of clinching a victory. Simultaneously is key here as some raffles have a small window of time in which you can enter. Each account operates independently, and the cumulative effect increases the buyers presence in the raffle, improving the odds of success.

To illustrate, envision a two-million-participant horse race where all the horses have an equal chance of winning. If you have twenty horses in the race and your competitor has just one, you inherently possess a higher chance of winning the race. In the context of releases, raffle botting allows for more entries, acting like having more horses in an equal race, enhancing the probability of securing the drop.

 Tip: Both types of botting require multiple profiles to increase your chances of success. It necessitates using several accounts with different information to maximise your chances of winning.

Considerations and Challenges

Websites facilitating drops or raffles deploy a multitude of sophisticated filters to prevent successes. These filters scrutinise:

1. Addresses (most common).
2. Phone Number.
3. Names.
4. Cards.
5. Device.
6. Wi-Fi.

Despite these measures, experienced bot users possess the expertise to navigate and overcome these challenges. While this chapter provides valuable insights for your botting journey, it's important to note that bot-specific guides offer tailored strategies for success. These specialised guides, often available online or through bot-specific cook groups, provide in-depth knowledge specific to the intricacies of each bot. In most cases, these resources are bundled in packages when the bot is purchased.

The Importance of Banking and Cards

In botting, having a secure bank with the right facilities is paramount. As briefly mentioned earlier, the use of multiple cards is essential for success, but this practice often encounters filters designed to detect identical cards. An effective solution to bypass this obstacle is the utilisation of Virtual Credit Cards (**VCCs**). These virtual counterparts operate similarly to normal debit or credit cards but are connected to a single bank account. Platforms like Revolut exemplify this concept, enabling a user to generate up to twenty virtual debit cards. This approach streamlines the process, consolidating multiple cards while maintaining funds in one centralised location, effectively evading filters. While Revolut serves as a specific example, various other methods and platforms cater to different setups and scales.

This method is applicable to both credit and debit cards and works similarly with just the normal differences between them. The example Revolut, as previously stated, can allow a user to generate up to twenty debit cards for free. This is great for someone starting to bot but can be used in collaboration with others listed below for those with a very advanced setup. The US offers a wider range of options, with more platforms providing virtual and physical cards. Availability varies by country. Some are for free, some are offered for a one-time purchase and some with a monthly subscription model.

As with everything in the digital world, things are ever-changing, staying clued up is among the best things you can do. Doing thorough research for each card provider is essential to understand how they work. Watch

YouTube guides, read up on the details, and join cook groups to enhance your understanding.

Card Providers and Generation Methods

1. Curve Card.
2. Multiple Highstreet Banks.
3. Monese.
4. Monzo.
5. Revolut.
6. iCard.
7. American Express.

These are UK providers and can change by the day.

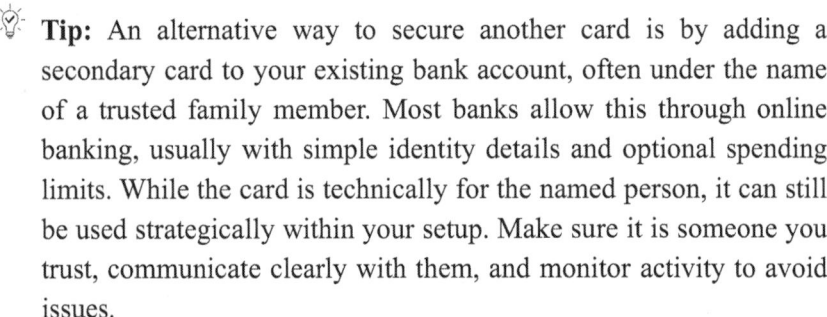 **Tip:** An alternative way to secure another card is by adding a secondary card to your existing bank account, often under the name of a trusted family member. Most banks allow this through online banking, usually with simple identity details and optional spending limits. While the card is technically for the named person, it can still be used strategically within your setup. Make sure it is someone you trust, communicate clearly with them, and monitor activity to avoid issues.

Cards and bank accounts are arguably the most important elements of the process as they facilitate successful checkouts.

Tip: For resellers under eighteen, seeking permission before using family members' cards for transactions is essential. Platforms like eBay require users to be eighteen, and they can detect if a card belongs to a minor. By involving family and obtaining permission, you ensure a secure and smooth financial process for transferring earnings, avoiding potential issues.

Finances

Effective financial management is necessary for success. Whether you are a novice or an experienced botter, understanding the costs involved is paramount. We will get into the various expenses associated with running a bot, ensuring a clear understanding of all financial considerations. Let us explore an example of a set up and crunch the numbers to see how botting can be worth your while.

Prudence

Prudence is a fundamental concept in finance that advocates for a cautious and realistic approach when dealing with numerical data. Its primary objective is to ensure a careful consideration of potential losses, thereby promoting a more accurate representation of one's financial standing. Adopting prudence proves advantageous as it encourages the recognition of possible losses in a timely manner. This approach involves erring on the side of caution, such as slightly inflating costs or rounding down figures.

For instance, if a product is sold for £63, a prudent approach might involve recording it as £60. While the actual profit remains £63, this practice prevents the overestimation of profits or revenues, consequently avoiding unnecessary strain on a project or business.

Assumptions

- You are a relatively new botter.
- Your aim is to run twenty entries.
- Cost calculated at time of writing.
- You are using the bot **USNKRS.**

Bot Cost

Understanding the financial environment begins with evaluating the cost of the bot itself. For this example, USNKRS, at the time of writing requires a subscription fee of £200 for a six-month period. Adopting a prudent approach, this rounds up to about £35 per month.

173

Virtual Cards

Some card providers require a subscription, for this the earlier example of Revolut is perfect as it offers twenty VCCs for free. Its best to opt for a cost-effective solution which saves capital and mitigates additional expenses, aligning with our prudent financial strategy.

Nike Accounts

Navigating the Nike ecosystem necessitates having twenty individual Nike accounts. While one could create these accounts manually, opting to purchase twenty Nike accounts is a pragmatic choice in this scenario. This incurs a one-time payment, with prices as of 2023, ranging from £20 to £40 per twenty, influenced by factors such as bulk buying discounts.

Nike accounts are essential for this particular bot, which is specifically designed for the Nike SNKRS app. This is common with most bots, as they are typically tailored to work with a specific app or website. Only a select few bots are versatile enough to operate across multiple platforms or websites.

Proxies

A proxy is a server that acts as an intermediary between a user's device and the internet, allowing for anonymous browsing and masking the user's IP address. You do not need to understand proxies that well to be able to use them effectively.

The importance of proxies in masking identities and accessing various locations cannot be overstated in botting. Managing twenty bots requires an equal number as they are assigned to each account, typically priced at around £25 to £40 for twenty. Proxies usually need to be renewed monthly.

Proxies serve as a vital investment in the botting infrastructure. Cook groups and botting groups, give advice and offers regarding proxies.

Calculating Costs:

Summarising the financial outlay, the total cost encompasses the bot itself over six months (£200), monthly proxies (£30 x 6 = £180), and the one-time expenditure on Nike accounts (£40). The total cost for this six-month venture approximates around £420. Breaking even on this investment requires a monthly profit of around £70. This calculation is based on the premise of a beginner botter aiming to offset the initial costs over the six-month period.

This setup, while relatively cost-effective for beginners, assumes an ideal scenario were hitting one sought-after sneaker release per month is feasible. Importantly, achieving this breakeven point without even having a botting setup is plausible but may present challenges.

In the context of a highly anticipated Nike release, it's conceivable to recoup costs in a single drop by securing multiple pairs. However, the unpredictable nature of releases and the potential for setbacks, especially for beginners, requires a level of caution and tempered expectations. Exercise prudence and recognise that success is not guaranteed, particularly in the initial stages. Embrace the learning curve during the first six months, leveraging both successes and setbacks to refine your strategies and adapt to botting. The journey is an invaluable educational experience, laying the groundwork for a more informed approach in subsequent endeavours.

Acquisition

The goal of botting obviously lies in the successful acquisition and resale of coveted shoes, aiming not only to recover costs but to turn a profit. This critical phase requires a well-considered budget to cover the expenses associated with purchasing the sneakers themselves.

For those operating with the described beginner botting setup, a recommended budget falls in the range of £1000 - £1500. This allocation is designed to strike a balance, providing the financial flexibility necessary to secure desirable releases while maintaining fiscal prudence.

Despite the smaller scale of this setup, the underlying principle remains consistent: budgeting is needed to optimise profit potential.

As the scale of your botting operation grows, so should your budget. In the case of an advanced botting setup involving hundred accounts, a suggested budget of £10,000 and beyond becomes needed due to the sheer size of the operation. This substantial budget aligns with the expanded scope and increased chances of success that come with a larger setup. However, with the amplified scale also comes a proportional increase in challenges and troubleshooting requirements. If you find yourself in this situation, be sure to revisit *Chapter Nine*, particularly the sections on taxes and incorporation, as they will be especially relevant.

As your budget expands, so do the complexities and potential risks within your operations. While a larger budget increases your chances of securing high-demand releases, it does introduce the risk of **diseconomies of scale**. With a more substantial setup, success becomes more critical, as the stakes are higher. Strike a balance between the size of your operation and the potential challenges it may entail.

 Tip: After recognising bots as valuable assets, the journey doesn't end with ownership. Platforms like Bot Mart present opportunities to rent, sell or swap bots, adding a layer of flexibility to a botter's financial strategy.

The Reality Check

Imagine a new botter had spent weeks preparing for his first drop. He had bought a well-reviewed bot, stocked up on proxies and set up multiple virtual cards. The setup created was clean. He had followed cook group advice down to the second. Yet after several drops, he had nothing to show for it but failed checkouts, cart errors and declined payments. His proxies had burned through his balance, server costs had stacked up and his accounts had been flagged. Each release became a source of stress. He had sunk over £400 with no successful checkouts, and the only thing growing was doubt.

This could be the reality of botting and it can feel like an endless pressure cooker. The financial costs build up fast and returns can be slow or inconsistent. This can be especially stressful after weeks of effort and investment.

To prevent this from becoming your reality, it is crucial to treat it seriously and take key steps to maximise your chances of success. Many fail not because the tools are poor, but because they are unprepared or cut corners, so following these guidelines can help save time, money and motivation.

Have the necessary capital - As discussed earlier in the chapter, you need to go into botting with a clear understanding of the financial risks. Make sure you have at least the recommended amounts, and ideally more, because if things do not go your way understand you could lose both money and time.

Do your due diligence - Watch setup videos, read guides specific to your bot and understand every aspect of your setup before running it on a real drop or even purchasing it.

Use all available resources - If you are in a cook group for a specific bot, use everything they provide. Read the guides, attend group calls, and do not hesitate to speak with admins or experienced members for help.

Keep detailed logs - Track your errors, success rates, proxy performance and card declines. Over time, this will help you identify what is working and what is not so you can adjust.

Stay updated - Botting environments shift constantly. Platforms change their security, payment processors update rules, and bots receive patches. Keep on top of these updates to avoid running an outdated or ineffective setup.

Botting is a proper grind. If you are not serious, do not have the time, or lack the energy and funds to commit, it is not for you. This is not a casual hustle, it is a technical, high-pressure side business that demands your full focus.

Beyond the emotional and financial strain, there can be deeper risks involved. Ones that can impact your access, accounts and even your long-term ability to operate in the space. Before diving in, you need to understand not just how botting works, but the consequences it can bring.

Risk

Botting in general carries significant risks that extend beyond the initial financial investment. While botting is not illegal, it exists in a legal grey area. Most individuals engaging in botting are not committing a crime, but they are usually breaking the terms of service of the platforms involved. Legal action is extremely unlikely for small-scale botting but once it is done at a large scale meaning hundreds or even thousands of transactions it can attract serious legal scrutiny especially if it involves fraud or other criminal activity however even smaller operations are not without potential consequences

Retailers and platforms often implement bans against users who are detected botting. These can include standard account bans, IP bans that prevent access from a specific internet connection, or even device bans that block purchases from a specific phone or laptop. In some cases, users may find that delivery addresses are blacklisted altogether. If a user gets banned, the money spent on bots, proxies, servers, and accounts often becomes a sunk cost with little to no chance of recovery.

A key issue with botting is the lack of transparency. In many cases, users are not explicitly told that they have been banned or blocked. Instead, they might be silently filtered out — everything appears to function normally, but entries never win, and checkouts consistently fail. This leaves users stuck in a loop of failed attempts, unaware of the root cause.

Ethics

Botting is part of the wider reselling world where having better information and faster access gives you an advantage. Like flipping, restoring or spotting overlooked products to make a profit, botting is about using what you know and the tools available to get ahead. In business, if you do not take that advantage, someone else will.

Botting creates frustration for regular customers who miss out because bots buy stock faster. This is an ethical reality you must accept if you choose to use these methods. Reselling can be a tough business. It rewards those who are informed, prepared and ready to act quickly.

At its core, reselling is about making the most of imperfect information and opportunities in a market where not everyone has equal access. Botting intensifies this but is not fundamentally different in principle. It is business and the aim is to profit by being smarter and faster.

It is important to respect clear ethical lines, such as avoiding harm to others or engaging in fraud. Crossing those lines risks more than just your reputation, it can end your business.

In Closing

We have covered the full botting process, from setting up accounts and proxies to techniques like j1gging and managing multiple cards, hopefully providing a fair overview of the reality. Botting is complex, challenging and not a guaranteed path to success. It demands skill, constant learning and careful risk management. If you choose to use botting, remember it is just one part of a much bigger business.

The methods you have learned here are tools to be used wisely and responsibly. Success comes not from shortcuts or cheating but from understanding the game, respecting your market and working hard to stay ahead without crossing ethical or legal boundaries. Even then, nothing is guaranteed. If you choose to engage in botting, do so with a clear understanding of the risks, a willingness to adapt and the patience to deal with setbacks.

Chapter Summary

❖ We covered what botting is, why it is used, the benefits it offers and the key terms and strategies involved in the process.

❖ We introduced the concept of jigging, it's role in avoiding bot detection, the details it alters, and the serious issues it can cause, highlighting why it is a risky and often discouraged method.

❖ There are two main types of botting: drop and raffle botting, both requiring multiple accounts and cards to bypass filters.

❖ Using virtual or additional cards helps improve success, with careful setup and monitoring essential to avoid issues.

❖ We broke down the finances, associated costs and risks involved in running a botting operation.

PART 4

Beer Money

Chapter Thirteen

Beer Money

Beer Money: Refers to the easy money that can be made online through various simple methods. The term comes from the idea of making enough money to cover casual expenses, like buying a beer.

I am not affiliated with any company mentioned and do not profit from sharing this information.

But beer money can be more than that. It might cover your next takeaway or trip to KFC with friends, but it can also give you the starting capital to try something bigger. For many, it is a practical first step towards reselling, side hustles, or simply having a bit more breathing room.

Imagine This

You are sixteen or seventeen, forced into college doing a course you do not particularly care about just because it seemed like the only option. You have £0 to your name. Your parents cannot help you. They say college is the best thing for you, but it does not help when you are sat there every day with a packed lunch, watching everyone else head to KFC or Subway. There is nothing wrong with bringing your own food, but sometimes you just want to fit in, or at least have the option to. You want to start doing something, anything

You have tried to get a job, but no one is hiring. You have no qualifications, no experience, no car and no real time outside of education yet. Maybe you applied for JD, for Asda, even to wait tables, but still nothing. You feel stuck. You know you want more. You want to make your first move.

Maybe it is flipping your first pair of trainers, buying and selling bundles of PlayStation games, or setting up a Vinted page. Maybe it is getting enough capital to unlock a cashback run, join a cook group, or start a vending machine hustle. But right now, even buying the first item feels impossible.

You do not need a job.

You do not need funding.

You just need a start.

And you can get it online, with no capital, through beer money methods.

This chapter starts the final section of the book, focusing on simple ways to make money online that anyone can begin without special skills or upfront costs. It is an introductory look at beer money methods, giving you the foundation before moving into specific platforms and strategies in the chapters that follow. These methods require only your time, patience, and the ability to follow instructions. Some offers take just minutes, others can be repeated daily. None will make you rich overnight, but many can help you quickly earn your first £200–£300,enough to kickstart a side hustle or cover small expenses that help you feel connected and included.

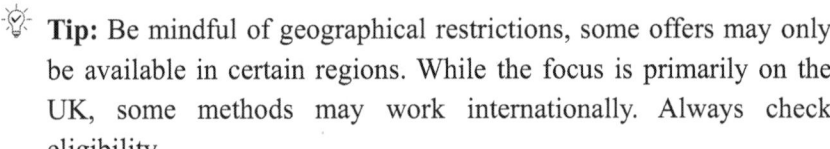 **Tip:** Be mindful of geographical restrictions, some offers may only be available in certain regions. While the focus is primarily on the UK, some methods may work internationally. Always check eligibility.

You can do this yourself or recommend it to friends and family as an easy way to earn some quick and low effort cash. Whether you are under or over eighteen, there is real value in getting your household involved. Some offers require you to be over eighteen, so if you are younger, ask an older sibling, cousin or parent to help. As discussed with Jack and Jane in Chapter Nine, this can make certain strategies more accessible. But even if you are old enough to sign up alone, do not stop there. Spread the love. Get the whole family on board. There is no reason you cannot double, triple or even quadruple your earnings by working together. Everyone benefits, and it can make a real difference when none of you are starting with much.

Maximising Beer Money Opportunities

- **Read the terms.** Always check the fine print. Look out for country restrictions, age limits, payout conditions, and minimum thresholds. Especially important if you are outside the UK or under eighteen. Never assume anything.

- **Keep track.** Use your notes app or a spreadsheet to record every offer you try, what you need to do, what you earned, and when you expect the payout. It helps avoid mistakes and lets you spot which strategies work best over time.

- **Stack and diversify.** Do not just focus on one site or app. Run several offers at once, and where possible, layer them. Cashback on top of a referral bonus? Perfect. Spreading across platforms keeps your earnings consistent.

- **Stick to the easy wins.** Focus on offers that are clear and quick. Avoid ones that are overly complicated or require too much personal data unless you fully understand the terms.

- **Withdraw when you can.** As soon as you meet the cash-out threshold, take the money. Do not leave it sitting in an app or account where you might forget about it or lose access.

- **Manage your capital.** If you are borrowing small amounts to fund offers or tasks, pay it back quickly. And if you earn a little extra, be the one who treats someone else. That goodwill goes a long way.

- **Make it count.** Whether you are flipping PlayStation bundles, setting up a Vinted page, or unlocking a cashback run, treat beer money as your starting fuel. It gets you moving.

Whether you are stacking pounds to launch a side hustle or just want a few extra treats each week, this is one of the easiest wins you can go for. To discover even more ways to make money, explore online forums like Reddit's r/beermoney and r/beermoneyuk. While r/beermoney is more US-focused, it still offers useful insights for international readers, and r/beermoneyuk focuses specifically on UK-based opportunities. Both communities share the latest deals, tips and earning strategies to help you stay ahead of the curve.

Chapter summary

❖ Beer money is the best money.

Chapter Fourteen

Bank Switches

In personal finance, individuals are always on the lookout for opportunities to increase their earnings. Bank switcher offers are a compelling way for those seeking to make the most of incentives provided by banks. This guide sheds light on what these offers entail, why banks deploy them, and how you can leverage them to your advantage.

Banking switcher offers are promotional incentives provided by banks to entice individuals to switch their accounts from one bank to another. These offers often come in the form of cash rewards, bonuses or other financial perks.

Banks launch switcher offers as a strategic move to attract new customers and increase their market share. By providing attractive incentives, they aim to lure individuals away from their current banking relationships.

For consumers, banking switcher offers represent an opportunity to earn extra cash or benefits by simply switching their accounts. This can include receiving a cash bonus or enjoying reduced fees and enhanced services.

Switcher offers vary across banks, each with its own requirements. These may include a minimum deposit, a set number of direct debits, a spending threshold, holding the account for a set time, or not having had an account with the bank recently. Always read the terms carefully. If you hold products like mortgages or loans with the bank, switching could complicate things and even cancel out the value of the offer. Check with your bank first. On the other hand, if you only use your current account for everyday spending, switching is usually straightforward and low-risk.

To see how a typical bank switch works in practice, let us walk through a real example step by step by breaking down exactly what you would need to do to qualify, meet the conditions and claim the reward.

Example: NatWest £200 Switcher Offer

Conditions:

- Minimum number of direct debits; In this case two.
- Closing another bank account to switch to NatWest through the current account switch service.
- Deposit of £1250.
- Completed within sixty days of opening account.
- Must not be existing NatWest customer

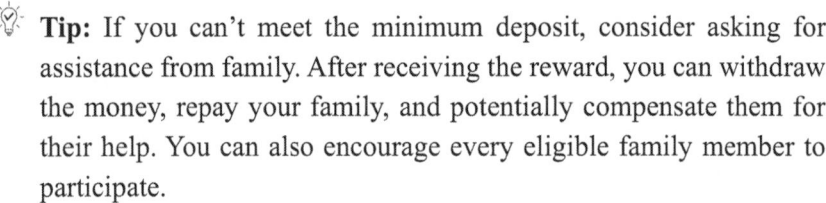 **Tip:** If you can't meet the minimum deposit, consider asking for assistance from family. After receiving the reward, you can withdraw the money, repay your family, and potentially compensate them for their help. You can also encourage every eligible family member to participate.

Step-by-Step

1. **Create a Spare Bank Account:** Begin by establishing a spare bank account with any financial institution. This account will be the one you switch. This will prevent disruptions with your primary account, avoiding issues with direct debits, card payments and regular transactions.
2. **Identify Lucrative Offers:** Research and identify banks offering attractive switcher offers. In this case the NatWest £200 switcher offer.
3. **Meet Requirements:** Ensure that you fulfil all specified requirements for the switch, such as maintaining a minimum deposit or setting up a certain number of direct debits.
4. **Initiate the Switch:** Use your spare bank account to switch to the chosen bank and complete the process through the Current Account Switch Service.

5. **Claim Your Reward:** Successfully execute the switch and receive the switcher offer reward, in this example, £200.

6. **Flexible Options:** If desired, switch back to your old bank account or choose to remain with the new bank, all while keeping your original account intact.

7. **Patience:** Switching current accounts can be a process that takes several days, and in some cases, even weeks, so exercise patience throughout.

☼ **Tip:** Deposits for bank switches are absolutely harmless. You can withdraw the money at any time and you will not lose anything. It is simply a condition you need to meet.

Remember, this is an example. The actual execution of switcher offers may involve more intricacies. Conduct thorough research, tailor your approach to each offer's unique conditions, and use easy to find online guides for a more detailed understanding of each individual offer.

☼ **Tip:** Reuse the secondary bank account to switch multiple times instead of opening and closing new accounts repeatedly. This allow for you to claim multiple offers while keeping things simple.

Common Pitfalls

Not Meeting Conditions

Be sure to meet the switch conditions. Each bank has its own terms, such as direct debits, deposit amounts or card spending. Read the terms carefully and check the offer requirements to ensure you qualify for the bonus.

Credit Score

Be aware that switching can temporarily lower your credit score. It usually recovers within a few months, but if you are planning to apply for a mortgage, loan, or credit card soon, consider holding off. Some banks run hard credit checks, which can negatively affect your rating.

Direct Debits

When switching bank accounts for a switching bonus, many people forget to set up their direct debits. This can cost you the bonus entirely. Some offers now require two or more active direct debits to be set up and paid out from the new account. It is important to understand how to set up, manage and cancel to use them to your advantage.

If you are unsure where to start, r/beermoneyuk is a helpful resource for setting up direct debits. It lists fast and low-cost options, often £1 or less, that meet switching requirements and can usually be set up within a few days. This allows you to qualify for a switch bonus quickly.

Another route is setting up direct debits to charities. These usually take a bit longer to process but can be a meaningful option if you are happy to give back.

 Tip: Most direct debits take around seven working days to set up, so once you've initiated them, you may need to wait before completing the switch.

Direct debits can slightly eat into your profit. But think of it like this: if you spend £5 to activate two and earn £100 or more in return, that's still a massive return on investment.

Always double-check that:

- The direct debits are active and visible in your new account and they've successfully been paid at least once.
- If you do not plan to switch again, cancel any unnecessary direct debits after receiving your bonus to avoid pointless payments.
- Be mindful of deadlines and account setup times. If an offer expires in six days, you likely won't have enough time to set up and meet the requirements. Plan ahead to avoid missing out on the bonus.

Bank Accounts

Always use the official current account switching service to ensure a smooth transition and qualify for the bonus.

Some offers are only for new customers or those who haven't held an account with the bank in a certain period.

 Tip: Some banks charge a monthly fee to maintain certain accounts. For example, Lloyds charges £3 per month for its Club Lloyds account. After receiving your switch bonus, make sure to either switch again, downgrade to a free account, or close the account altogether to avoid unnecessary fees.

By following these steps and avoiding common mistakes, you can take full advantage of bank switching offers and turn them into a reliable source of money.

Wrapping Up

Here's a snapshot of switcher offers in recent years as of May 2025 to show what's possible You can walk friends, partners or family members through the process, or complete it for them, to make sure everyone benefits.

- NatWest Bank: £200.
- Barclays Bank: £175.
- Lloyds Bank: £175.
- First Direct: £175.
- Nationwide: £175.
- Santander: £150.
- Co-operative Bank: £150.
- TSB Bank: £100.

Some people have even claimed the same offer multiple times by using different emails and phone numbers. However, banks state these deals are for new customers or those who have not had an account recently, so repeat claims are not guaranteed and may be slightly risky.

While there might only be a few offers available at once, new ones usually appear when others end. Keeping a spare account open just for switching makes it easier to act quickly. You can prepare it in advance with the necessary requirements so you are ready when the next deal launches.

If you want to stay ahead of the curve, regularly check sites like MoneySavingExpert and Scrimpr alongside the r/beermoneyuk Reddit page, which keep up-to-date lists of the latest bank switch offers and help explain the terms and intricacies in plain English.

Done right, bank switching can be one of the easiest and most repeatable ways to earn a few hundred quid extra every year. It is not a get-rich-quick scheme, but it is one of the most reliable ways to pocket free money with minimal effort. If you stay organised and take a consistent approach, those hundreds can really add up over time.

With a bit of preparation and the right timing, you are just one smooth switch away from easy wins and extra cash in your account.

Chapter Summary

❖ Bank switcher offers provide an opportunity for consumers to earn cash or benefits by switching accounts, with banks offering these incentives to attract new customers and expand their market share, but it is important to carefully review terms and conditions.

❖ We walk through the example of the NatWest £200 switcher offer, detailing the steps to take, the requirements to meet, how to ensure success and common pitfalls to avoid.

❖ Bank switching is a repeatable and low-effort way to earn hundreds each year by staying organised, understanding the requirements and using a secondary account to take advantage of ongoing offers as they appear.

Chapter Fifteen

Sign Ups and Referrals

Another easy way to earn quick cash is through referral and sign-up schemes. These are commonly offered by banks, alternative banking apps and investment platforms, rewarding users for joining or referring others. Banks like Revolut offer referral bonuses, which we will explore in detail in this chapter.

This chapter will also use stock platforms to demonstrate how these schemes work. These platforms often provide free shares or small payouts, which, when combined with bank promotions, offer a reliable, low-effort method to earn extra income.

Geographical restrictions may apply.

Referral schemes are offered for a similar reason as switch offers, to help to increase the platforms user base and incentivise people to use their service. Offering rewards for referrals is one way to do this.

We will focus on Revolut as an example. Launched in 2015, Revolut has become renowned for its innovative banking services. Beyond traditional features, the platform offers users an opportunity to earn through its referral scheme, contributing to the growth of its user community.

Step-by-Step Example

1: First sign up to Revolut yourself and make a qualifying transaction of at least £1. This unlocks the £20 sign up bonus.

2: Next refer a friend to Revolut through your unique referral link.

3: Instruct your friend to do the following:

- Add funds to their account via a debit card or bank transfer.
- Order a physical card.
- Make three purchases, each with a minimum value of £5. Certain transactions, such as gambling, gift cards or transfers may not qualify. Weird spacing sort out Completion of these steps within the specified time frame, typically spanning a couple of months, ensures eligibility for rewards.

Tip: Advise your friend to utilise the card for purchases they would have made regardless. This way, they gain from the process without incurring additional expenses.

4: After completion of these steps, you and your referee should be rewarded. Do remember that promotional rewards can vary widely. Some offer fixed amounts for both you and your friends, while others provide random sums between £10 - £200. Always stay updated on the latest promotion details.

While this guide focuses solely on Revolut, referral schemes across banks are constantly changing. Use this as a flexible framework, not a fixed rulebook. Always research current terms to ensure you are making the most of the latest offers.

Banks are often the first-place people look for referral opportunities, though a growing number of digital platforms, particularly in the financial space, now offer similar incentives for signing up or referring others. Stock and investment apps are a prime example. These platforms provide another low-effort way to earn quick rewards, often in the form of free shares or small cash bonuses. With the right approach, they can complement bank offers and help boost your capital even further.

Referral Bonuses on Stock Platforms

The next method we will explore centres around stock trading platforms, each equipped with referral schemes like those observed with banks. Our primary focus will be on Trading 212, recognised as one of the leading platforms for stocks and shares in the UK.

To clarify this chapter does not dive into stock trading itself. It focuses solely on referral schemes which essentially translates to low effort income.

The steps we will discuss are not only applicable to Trading 212 and also extend to other popular trading apps in the UK, such as Free Trade and Wombat.

Although the core processes remain similar, these platforms might introduce tiny, intricate details that distinguish them. Referral schemes, much like those in banking, are subject to change and may carry geographical restrictions. While Trading 212 consistently offers this promotion, keep in mind that such offerings may evolve, and it is advisable to stay informed.

 Tip: Many promotions impose a maximum number of referrals per person, usually capped at around five per period. Knowing these limits is vital for participation and yielding your overall benefits.

1: Open a Trading 212 account. Stock platforms like this often offer a sign-up bonus such as a free share worth up to £100 when you start trading with as little as £1.

 Tip: Make sure to check for sign-up bonuses or referrals before joining any financial platform, as there is usually an easy reward to claim.

2: Upon opening your Trading 212 account, undergo the necessary identity verification process. Subsequently, deposit funds into your account, meeting the minimum amount required. As of 2025, the minimum deposit stands at £1.

3: Invest your £1 in a share. Any share, it does not matter which.

4: Extend the opportunity to a friend by inviting them to join Trading 212 using your invite link which can be found within the app. Advice the person you referred to follow steps 1-3 as you have.

Upon successful completion of the steps by your referred friend, both of you will receive a share with a value ranging from £10 to £100. While the expectation should be modest, around £10-£20, it will add to your capital.

5: As the referrer, you can withdraw your share immediately, but your friend must exercise patience and leave their free share untouched for a month before being eligible to withdraw.

💡 **Tip:** Remind your friend to set a notification for a month to ensure they don't overlook their potential earnings.

To maximise your capital increase, repeat steps 1-5 with different friends. The maximum amount per period is five friends. This will bring in a minimum of £50. Importantly, remember that your friends can also refer others once they have joined, creating a chain of potential earnings.

💡 **Tip:** Both the Revolut and Trading 212 referral schemes are reset periodically, allowing you to repeat the process multiple times. Period lengths can vary, so stay vigilant.

Responsible Investing

Before engaging in referral schemes on stock platforms, it is essential to understand the risks involved, including potential financial loss. If you are new to stock trading, proceed with caution. This guide focuses on leveraging referral bonuses with minimal financial exposure, not on encouraging stock trading.

While it's possible to earn rewards with just a £1 commitment, the goal is to claim the referral bonus and withdraw quickly. Actual stock trading carries significant risks, especially for beginners, and it is strongly discouraged to invest substantially with no experience.

Our focus is on taking advantage of referral incentives without getting caught up in long-term trading or speculation. For those inexperienced in stock trading, it is strongly recommended to refrain from making investment decisions and to seek advice from financial professionals if it is something you are interested.

 Tip: Some referral schemes rely on help from friends or family, which is completely fine. However, do not pester or pressure anyone into taking part. If someone tells you they are not interested or seem hesitant, respect their response and move on. You can explain the benefits once, especially if it is mutually rewarding, but always read the room. Being polite and considerate will get you further than pushing too hard.

Next Move

Referral and sign-up schemes, alongside bank switch offers, provide an easy and effective way to bolster your capital with minimal effort. By leveraging online resources, such as a simple Google search, you can quickly find the latest offers that could see you earning rewards for spending or investing small amounts. Some offers, like those from high street banks, can range from £20 to £50 for fulfilling basic requirements such as spending £10 or referring a friend.

If you are smart about combining referrals, sign-ups, and bank switches throughout the year, you could easily make a couple of thousand pounds with little to no risk. The process is straightforward and requires careful attention to the terms and conditions, ensuring you can fulfil the requirements.

The money you earn through these schemes can be used in many ways, whether that's investing in reselling, starting a business, investing in stocks or simply treating yourself to something nice. It's quick cash with minimal risk, making it an accessible and low-effort way to increase your capital. Keep building up your funds, and with some strategic planning, you can easily see the benefits of these schemes over time.

Chapter Summary

❖ Sign-up and referral offer easy cash bonuses.

❖ We walk through step-by-step examples across various niches that offer referral and sign-up bonuses, outlining the necessary steps and key considerations for ensuring success.

❖ Responsible investing is crucial, as stock trading carries significant risks, and these opportunities should be used to boost capital, not for speculative investments.

Chapter Sixteen

Side Gigs

This chapter is about squeezing every drop of value out of what is already available. It focuses on overlooked methods that can generate money again without taking real risks.

These are not get-rich-quick schemes. They are structured systems designed to help build financial momentum through consistent use. If used smartly, they can build momentum from nothing and turn small wins into a solid financial foundation. Most of the methods require no special skills and some need almost no starting capital. The real key is consistency, focus and knowing which order to do things in.

Cashback and Reward Apps

Cashback platforms are not just about saving money on shopping. Many of them offer rewards for tasks like signing up for services, trying out apps or referring other users. This is a way to earn a bit of extra cash by completing offers, some quick and some more involved, while knowing which ones are worth your time.

Why They Exist

Retailers Want Traffic. Retailers are constantly trying to get more eyes on their products and services. By working with cashback platforms, they pay a small fee for each customer that buys something, rather than spending blindly on ads that may or may not convert. It's performance-based advertising, they only pay when they make money.

Shoppers Want Incentive. Cashback is a no-brainer for shoppers. You are getting a percentage of your spend back on stuff you were planning to buy anyway. It turns everyday purchases into a small income stream.

The Sites Profit Too. These platforms earn affiliate commission from retailers. The clever bit is, they share a good chunk of it with you while keeping a slice for themselves. With thousands of users and purchases flying through the site every day, the profits add up fast even if they're only keeping 10–20% per transaction.

How the Cashback Model Works

When you click a link on a cashback site to a retailer, the visit is tracked using a special affiliate ID. This tells the retailer exactly where the customer came from.

If you go on to make a purchase, the retailer pays the cashback site a commission for referring you — basically a digital finder's fee.

The cashback site then gives you a portion of that commission. Depending on the deal, this could be anywhere from 1% to 50% of your spend or even a fixed amount like £10 to £50 for certain offers, such as broadband signups or financial products.

The site takes a small share of the commission for itself. You get most of it, the site makes money and the retailer lands a customer. Everyone wins.

Task-Based Cashback

We will use CashbackUK as an example of how cashback websites operate. This platform rewards users for completing specific tasks. These can include:

- Downloading apps and completing conditions (e.g., reaching a level in a game or depositing a specified amount in an investment app).
- Entering prize draws or competitions.
- Starting free trials.
- Referring friends.

Fifteen-Level Task Model

CashbackUK uses a tiered system made up of fifteen levels. To unlock a withdrawal, you need to complete at least one task on each level. Some levels offer one or two options, while others have up to six or seven. The more tasks you complete, the more money you earn. After each task, the next level unlocks and your cashback balance increases.

Once you have completed at least one task on all 15 levels, you become eligible to withdraw your earnings.

These sites rely on breakage. Users starting tasks, reaching level seven or eight, then giving up or forget to complete all fifteen. If you don't complete all fifteen levels and hit the withdrawal threshold, your earnings sit there, unpaid. They've earned the commission, but you haven't cashed out.

They rely on you giving up before completing the process. Stay consistent and do not leave money on the table.

💡**Tip:** Reward values are usually based on how much cashback platforms get paid for each task, minus what they share with you. So higher-value tasks often involve more effort or risk.

Here's how a few levels might look:

Level One

- Refer a Friend – £5.
- Watch a 5-minute video – £3.

Complete either task to unlock Level Two.

Level Two

- Enter a £100 gift card giveaway – £10.
- Subscribe to a magazine for 99p/month – £0.50.

In this example, the magazine subscription isn't worth it and should be avoided.

Level Three

- Enter a draw for a dream car (£2 entry fee) – £14.
- Download a mobile game and reach level 4 – £6.

Tips for Maximising Earnings

Set Reminders: Some tasks have timers or expiry periods. Set phone reminders for when things unlock or trials need to be cancelled.

Use Common Sense: If a task pays £3 but requires spending £10 — skip it. Focus on net gain, not just high numbers.

Time vs. Value: Some tasks can take days or even weeks to complete. Decide if it's worth waiting or better to complete a smaller task and move on.

Be Methodical: Track what you've done, note down proof (screenshots, emails) and don't be afraid to contact support if something doesn't track properly.

Expectations

Time Commitment: Roughly 2–3 weeks to complete all levels, most of which is waiting for confirmations, unlocks or tasks to validate.

Support Contact: You will probably need to reach out to support for at least one or two tasks that don't track. Keep proof and emails handy. Resolution is usually straightforward.

Payout: Expect to make around £100–£200, depending on the tasks available when you join and how many you complete.

Once you understand how cashback and reward platforms work, the next step is to put that momentum into a structured plan. The Pathways section shows how to take these initial gains and turn them into larger, more strategic opportunities. It is where your casual side earnings start to become meaningful capital that can fund bigger ventures, whether that means reselling, investing, or growing another business idea.

Pathways

Phase 1

Begin with simple sign up offers such as Revolut or Trading 212. These financial platforms often give new customers small but instant rewards just for creating an account and meeting basic requirements, usually without needing any real capital. This makes them the best place to start when you are first building. Even with just £1 or £2, you can quickly grow it into £20 to £40, and sometimes more if you find a particularly good deal. These methods are ideal for anyone starting with almost nothing, as they give you a fast and low effort way to establish a foundation.

Phase 2

Once you have collected the initial sign-up rewards, the next logical step is referrals. Many of the same apps and platforms offer bonuses for inviting new users, so they naturally link together. Referrals are a simple way to build up extra beer money while also getting friends or family involved. At a basic level this can give you a steady trickle of income, but some people take it much further by scaling across multiple promotions or running referrals consistently over longer periods.

Phase 3

By this stage you should have enough built up from sign-ups and referrals to move on to cashback tasks. This is where the earnings can become more consistent and you can expect to make around a few hundred. Cashback sites reward you for completing offers and while some tasks take a little longer to clear, the payout is often worth the wait. At this point you are no longer just scraping together small sign-up bonuses but instead building a reliable base of beer money.

Phase 4

Once you have a couple of hundred pounds from earlier phases, the bigger opportunities open up through bank switches. These can drastically increase your capital, often adding hundreds at a time. If you already have savings or regular income, you can skip straight to this stage, but for someone starting from zero it makes more sense to treat bank switches as a later-phase upgrade once the earlier methods have helped to build your capital.

Phase 5

If you cannot yet meet the requirements for a bank switch, such as minimum deposits, do not force it. Instead, wait until you can or consider using family support, since families can multiply profits by switching together or on each other's behalf. Even if you decide not to use this money to kickstart a business, it is still worthwhile. Beer money gains can go toward personal goals such as a holiday, a home gym or even supporting a family project.

For those ready to move forward, this is the point where capital shifts from short-term earnings into something greater. The smaller methods have built momentum, and now the focus is on putting money to work through reselling, investing or starting another venture. By this stage you are no longer just scraping small wins but using money as a tool to create sustainable growth. Apply it to your hustle, whatever that may be. If you already have a job and savings, you can jump straight into this step, but for those starting from nothing, it makes sense to build gradually. Each step helps to fund the next and set you up for success.

Closing Thoughts

That said, this is a framework, not a rulebook. If you are already working or have savings, feel free to skip ahead and use higher-value strategies earlier or none at all and get straight into hustling. Some methods take time for lower payouts. If you think they are not worth the effort, you are free to leave them out. The point is not to follow every step perfectly but to move forward with clarity and to avoid wasting time on the wrong things at the wrong stage.

This approach builds income without risk and in a logical progression, designed for people starting from zero. You begin with tasks that need very little money, use the profits from those to unlock bigger methods, and compound your gains.

Use each step to set up the next. That is how you turn nothing into something and eventually, something into a lot more.

Chapter Summary

❖ Cashback and reward platforms provide small but steady earnings through sign-ups, tasks and referrals.

❖ The aim is to build momentum, turning small low risk wins into capital that can fund reselling, investing or other ventures.

Tips

Chapter Two: *Value*

☀ **Tip:** When starting out, use all available platforms and get a feel for them as a user. See how your product performs on each over time before tailoring your approach to specific platforms. With experience, you will develop intuition and start to recognise which platforms work best for your products and goals.

☀ **Tip:** Use the reminders and notes apps on your phone to track releases and set dates in your calendar to stay prepared.

Chapter Three: **Sourcing**

☀ **Tip:** When participating in the second-hand market, particularly in auction-style bidding, set alarms or reminders for auction end times. It is often possible to win bids by placing your offer just before the auction expires. This strategy, known as 'sniping,' can give you an edge in securing desirable items at competitive prices.

☀ **Tip:** Research upcoming auctions in your area or niche and sign up for email alerts. Many auction houses provide online catalogues beforehand, allowing you to identify potential opportunities in advance.

☀ **Tip:** To maximise success at conventions, arrive early and be prepared with cash, as many vendors prefer quick, hassle-free transactions. Also, consider bringing a price comparison app to ensure you are getting the best deals.

Chapter Four: **The Second-Hand Market**

☼ **Tip:** Weekends are peak browsing times on second-hand platforms. Upload your listings then and remain active to increase visibility and your chances of a quick sale.

☼ **Tip:** If, for any reason, doubt arises about the seller's possession of said item, a practical tip is to request a photo with the item featuring the current date and the seller's username. This additional layer of verification can be a valuable precautionary step.

Chapter Five: ***Photography***

☼ **Tip:** Avoid using the flash on your camera, as it can create harsh shadows. Instead, opt for soft, diffused lighting to ensure even illumination and minimise shadows.

Chapter Six: **Platforms**

☼ **Tip:** Exercise caution when utilising eBay's auction feature. Auctions may lead to your listings selling for less than their market value or even less than your original purchase price. Consider utilising fixed price listings or setting a reserve price to better control the selling price and protect the value of your items.

☼ **Tip:** If you are going to meet a buyer through Gumtree or Marketplace, always choose a public place or meet at your home with family nearby for added safety. Negative experiences are very rare in general, and if you follow this guide's advice, such as carefully screening buyers and trusting your judgment, they are unlikely to happen.

☼ **Tip:** Opting for the 24/7 InPost lockers available on Vinted can simplify your shipping process, eliminating the need for label printing and postage expenses.

Chapter Seven: **Sales**

- **Tip:** Avoid undercutting, as it can lead to bricking. Bricking happens when sellers keep lowering their prices to compete, flooding the market and driving the item's value down. When everyone undercuts each other, the price drops fast, and the item becomes harder to sell at a profit. Items that lose value this way are sometimes referred to as bricks.

- **Tip:** If you receive interest in an item on a platform with high fees, consider messaging the potential buyer and suggesting a purchase on a more favourable platform. While not every buyer may agree, it's worth trying to reduce your selling costs.

- **Tip:** Bundling is also a great way to shift slower-moving items by pairing them with more desirable stock.

Chapter Eight: **Shipping & Customer Service**

- **Tip:** When it comes to premium shipping options, whether that's FedEx, UPS, DPD or Royal Mail, you can usually pay extra for cover on high-value items, so you are compensated for the item's value if anything happens, like loss or theft. Always check the terms and maximum cover limits of your chosen courier to ensure full protection.

- **Tip:** To minimise trips, choose one or two specific days each week (depending on your volume of sales) to go to a locker or a post office. Instead of making daily trips with single parcels, consolidate your packages and go once a week with multiple parcels to save time.

- **Tip:** Keep packaging from items you've purchased. You can reuse packaging by turning it inside out, saving you money and increasing your profits. Packing peanuts and bubble wrap among other things can also be saved.

- **Tip:** Some sellers offer 'free shipping' by building the cost into the product price. Always question why someone would ship for free, since it still costs money. While you should watch out for this as a buyer, it can also be a clever tactic to use yourself when selling.

Chapter Nine: **Expansion**

Tip: Use cook groups and tools as part of a broader strategy. While they're invaluable resources, combining this knowledge with your own research and expertise will give you the ultimate edge.

Tip: Sometimes a seller may be trying to offload stock that did not sell as expected. Be cautious and follow the steps outlined in this guide before committing to bulk purchases.

Tip: Using a middleman like an admin within a verified cook group is generally safe, but be aware they may take a small fee, similar to payment processors like PayPal.

Tip: In everyday language the terms profit and income tend to get mixed up because they are used more loosely. In this context, when people say income, they may actually be referring to profit, even though in strict accounting terms they're different.

Tip: Whether you are engaged in reselling or simply clearing out items around the house, it is essential to maintain records. Even a basic list can be invaluable when calculating items sold, profit and revenue generated. Keeping organised records ensures accuracy and helps you stay on top of your finances.

Tip: Selling old items you own or things from around the house is a great way to start. It helps generate positive reviews and much-needed capital.

Chapter Eleven: **Restoration**

- ⚐ **Tip:** Building relationships within the sneaker community or your specific niche is crucial. By cultivating connections with fellow people in your niche, you can provide specialised services to them.

- ⚐ **Tip:** Using multiple UV lights can speed up the deoxidation process by providing more consistent coverage. However, this increases the overall cost and may require additional fans to manage heat, so balance efficiency with your budget and setup space.

- ⚐ **Tip:** When searching for components like lighting and fans for your ice box, consider exploring the second-hand market through different platforms and apply the precautions outlined in Chapter Four when engaging in transactions within the second-hand market.

- ⚐ **Tip:** If you are planning to use an ice box long-term, it is worth investing in higher-quality equipment upfront. While it may cost more initially, better equipment is more durable, energy-efficient and cost-effective over time. Higher-quality UV lights, for instance, may last longer and provide better results, leading to lower energy costs and better profits in the long run.

- ⚐ **Tip:** Leaving your sneakers in sunlight to 'ice' might seem like a free option, but it comes with risks like sole separation, damage or even theft. Investing in an ice box is a safer and more reliable method.

- ⚐ **Tip:** For further guidance on assembling the ice box, consider watching instructional videos on platforms like YouTube, which provide a visual representation of the process and can offer valuable insights to guide you in constructing your ice box effectively.

Chapter Twelve: **Bot Technology**

> **Tip:** For a secure botting approach without resorting to jigging, it's strongly advised to use real addresses with explicit permission from family, friends, or neighbours. Ensure a transparent and ethical collaboration, offering incentives for each received parcel.

> **Tip:** Many bots are not readily available on the market and often have waiting lists. It's advisable to stay informed about release schedules and join waiting lists promptly to increase your chances of obtaining a bot when it becomes available.

> **Tip:** Both types of botting require multiple profiles to increase your chances of success. It necessitates using several accounts with different information to maximise your chances of winning.

> **Tip:** An alternative way to secure another card is by adding a secondary card to your existing bank account, often under the name of a trusted family member. Most banks allow this through online banking, usually with simple identity details and optional spending limits. While the card is technically for the named person, it can still be used strategically within your setup. Make sure it is someone you trust, communicate clearly with them, and monitor activity to avoid issues.

> **Tip:** For resellers under eighteen, seeking permission before using family members' cards for transactions is essential. Platforms like eBay require users to be eighteen, and they can detect if a card belongs to a minor. By involving family and obtaining permission, you ensure a secure and smooth financial process for transferring earnings, avoiding potential issues.

> **Tip:** After recognising bots as valuable assets, the journey doesn't end with ownership. Platforms like Bot Mart present opportunities to rent, sell or swap bots, adding a layer of flexibility to a botter's financial strategy.

Chapter Thirteen: **Beer Money**

🔅 **Tip:** Be mindful of geographical restrictions, some offers may only be available in certain regions. While the focus is primarily on the UK, some methods may work internationally. Always check eligibility.

Chapter Fourteen: **Bank Switches**

🔅 **Tip:** If you can't meet the minimum deposit, consider asking for assistance from family. After receiving the reward, you can withdraw the money, repay your family, and potentially compensate them for their help. You can also encourage every eligible family member to participate.

🔅 **Tip:** Deposits for bank switches are absolutely harmless. You can withdraw the money at any time and you will not lose anything. It is simply a condition you need to meet.

🔅 **Tip:** Reuse the secondary bank account to switch multiple times instead of opening and closing new accounts repeatedly. This allow for you to claim multiple offers while keeping things simple.

🔅 **Tip:** Most direct debits take around seven working days to set up, so once you've initiated them, you may need to wait before completing the switch.

🔅 **Tip:** Some banks charge a monthly fee to maintain certain accounts. For example, Lloyds charges £3 per month for its Club Lloyds account. After receiving your switch bonus, make sure to either switch again, downgrade to a free account, or close the account altogether to avoid unnecessary fees.

🔅 **Tip:** Advise your friend to utilise the card for purchases they would have made regardless. This way, they gain from the process without incurring additional expenses.

🔅 **Tip:** Many promotions impose a maximum number of referrals per person, usually capped at around five per period. Knowing these limits is vital for participation and yielding your overall benefits.

Chapter Fifteen: **Sign Up and Referrals**

Tip: Advise your friend to utilise the card for purchases they would have made regardless. This way, they gain from the process without incurring additional expenses.

Tip: Many promotions impose a maximum number of referrals per person, usually capped at around five per period. Knowing these limits is vital for participation and yielding your overall benefits.

Tip: Make sure to check for sign-up bonuses or referrals before joining any financial platform, as there is usually an easy reward to claim.

Tip: Remind your friend to set a notification for a month to ensure they don't overlook their potential earnings.

Tip: Both the Revolut and Trading 212 referral schemes are reset periodically, allowing you to repeat the process multiple times. Period lengths can vary, so stay vigilant.

Tip: Some referral schemes rely on help from friends or family, which is completely fine. However, do not pester or pressure anyone into taking part. If someone tells you they are not interested or seem hesitant, respect their response and move on. You can explain the benefits once, especially if it is mutually rewarding, but always read the room. Being polite and considerate will get you further than pushing too hard.

Chapter Sixteen: **Extras**

Tip: Reward values are usually based on how much cashback platforms get paid for each task, minus what they share with you. So higher-value tasks often involve more effort or risk.

Final Tip: Tips only work when acted on. Highlight or save those most relevant to your current phase and revisit them regularly. Execution matters more than memorization.

Glossary

This glossary provides definitions and explanations of key terms frequently throughout the guide and within the wider reselling community.

(SKU) Number: A stock keeping unit which uniquely identifies each product, serving as a reference code for inventory management.

Backdooring: When employees, often in big retail stores or the retailer themselves, exploit their positions to gain exclusive access to limited releases before they officially hit the shelves, usually for financial gain.

Beater: A sneaker that is worn daily, regardless of weather conditions, and is not cared for if it gets dirty.

Beer money: Easy money that can be made online through various simple methods. The term originates from the idea of earning small amounts of money to cover personal expenses, like drinks, hence 'beer money'.

BNIB: Brand new in box.

Botting: Using computer programs to help resellers quickly purchase highly sought-after products online, increasing their chances of securing a pair or multiple pairs.

Brick flips: Resellers selling products for less than they paid or at a small profit due to changes in demand or other factors.

Bricks: Sneakers that are difficult to sell or have low demand, resulting in resellers not making the expected profit.

Capital: The money or resources you have available to use for investment, trading or building income.

Colourway: A combination of colours used to distinguish different styles.

Cook Group: A community or online membership providing valuable information, tips, and insights to help resellers.

Copping: Successfully acquiring a coveted product, like scoring a win in the reselling game.

Diseconomies of scale: Happens when a business becomes so large that producing each unit costs more due to inefficiency.

Drops/Drop: A limited and highly anticipated release of a specific model by a brand or retailer.

DS: Deadstock, brand new or something that has never been worn.

Economies Of Scale: Economies of scale refer to the cost benefits a company experiences when increasing production, as the average cost to produce each unit becomes lower.

Fakes: Unauthorised copies of genuine sneaker that attempt to imitate the original design and branding. Fakes are typically of lower quality and lack the authenticity of genuine sneakers.

Flaking: Someone who backs out of a deal last minute, either as a buyer or seller.

Flip: Refers to the act of buying at retail or below market prices and reselling them in the secondary market at higher prices to make a profit.

GR: General Release.

GS: Grade School sizes, designed for older kids and adolescents with smaller feet.

Hype: The driving force behind excitement and anticipation for a product, creating a ripple effect that influences demand and ultimately impacts value.

Hypebeasts: Those who follow popular trends and buy what's currently in demand without having their own distinct taste.

Ice Box: A device that you will need to assemble to ice the soles of your sneakers, restoring them to their original colour.

Icing: The sole icing process is a restorative technique that breathes new life into worn-out sneakers, bringing them closer to their original pristine condition. It effectively reverses the yellowing of the outsole, restoring it to its former white or icy state, hence the term icing.

Jigging: Resellers changing their address with purposeful spelling errors to make it seem they have multiple addresses.

LC: Legit Check.

Leaking: Refers to the unauthorised or unintended release of information, substances, or materials.

LTD: An abbreviation for 'Limited' usually used to describe a private limited company.

OG: Original release of a sneaker.

OOS: Out of stock.

PLC: Public Limited Company

Proxies: Secret weapons that help resellers bypass online retailer restrictions and increase their chances of successfully buying by giving them the appearance of being in different places at one singular time.

PS: Preschool sizes, made for younger children, typically aged 3 to 5 years old.

Replica (Reps): Replicas, commonly referred to as 'reps,' are imitations of popular apparel that aim to resemble their authentic counterparts.

Resell Price: The amount at which products are sold in the secondary market, usually higher than the original retail price. Resellers aim to make a profit by selling at this price.

Reseller: Someone who purchases at retail prices and sells them for a higher price in the secondary market, capitalising on the demand for exclusive or hard-to-find items

Restock: A pair that has previously dropped but is now available with new supply or stock.

Retail Price: The price set by retailers, which is the final selling price for customers.

Retailer: A business or person that sells goods to the public in relatively small quantities for use or consumption rather than for resale.

Retro: A re-release of an older sneaker.

Sample: One of the many prototypes that designs go through during production, usually not released to the public. Often rare and highly sought after by collectors.

SB: Skateboard.

Sneakerhead: A person who collects and trades sneakers as a hobby and has extensive knowledge about sneaker history.

Sole Sauce: A specially formulated deoxidising gel, often containing hydrogen peroxide, that is applied to yellowed sneaker soles to reverse oxidation and restore their original appearance during the sole icing process.

Sourcing: The process of finding and acquiring to add to your inventory.

TTS: True to Size.

UPC Codes: Universal Product Codes, integral to a recognised inventory system, providing a unique identification stamp for products on a global scale.

USNKRS: A premium UK-based bot designed to automate Nike releases, streamlining the checkout process for high-demand drops.

UV Light: UV light, or ultraviolet light, is a form of electromagnetic radiation with wavelengths shorter than visible light, often used in applications like sterilization, curing, and restoration due to its high-energy properties.

VCC: Virtual Credit Card.

W: 'W' stands for 'Women's' and indicates that the sneaker is available in women's sizes, not men's sizes.

WTS: Want to sell.

WTB: Want to buy.

WTT: Want to trade.

Enjoyed the book? Scan the QR code below to leave an honest review.
Your support is appreciated

https://www.amazon.co.uk/dp/B0FTZ7MFCW

Printed in Dunstable, United Kingdom